Editor
Lorin E. Klistoff, M.A.

Managing Editor
Karen Goldfluss, M.S. Ed.

Editor-in-Chief
Sharon Coan, M.S. Ed.

Cover Artist
Denise Bauer

Illustrator
Kevin McCarthy

Art Manager
Kevin Barnes

Art Director
CJae Froshay

Imaging
Rosa C. See

Product Manager
Phil Garcia

Publishers
Rachelle Cracchiolo, M.S. Ed.
Mary Dupuy Smith, M.S. Ed.

Develop Reading Fluency Using Poetry

Grades 2-4

• Literacy Activities   • Critical Thinking   • Comprehension

"Includes cloze activities"

Activity Page

The Sad Shoes

Using the description in the poem to help you, draw and color an illustration of the author's "Sad Shoes." Write a few sentences to go with your picture. In your sentences, explain why the shoes are sad, and why the author is sorry to see them go.

Author

Nan E. Hayes, M. Ed.

Teacher Created Materials, Inc.
6421 Industry Way
Westminster, CA
www.teachercreatedmaterials.com

ISBN-0-743...

©2004 Teacher Created Materials, Inc.

Made in U.S.A.

Table of Contents

Introduction

The need for high-interest supplemental reading materials veering from the norm and geared to motivate and inspire young readers has become apparent. From the valuable set of poems included in this book, activities were developed that motivate students and offer essential reading skill reinforcement at the same time.

The poems and ensuing activities are presented here. They offer valuable reinforcement in many essential reading skills, including letter-sound relationships, critical thinking, and comprehension. The students are lead easily to purposeful writing and reading fluency activities. Minimal planning and preparation is required of the teacher. The activities can be used as a supplement to any reading series and can be taught simultaneously to varying academic levels. In addition, many of the themes can be integrated for interdisciplinary purposes.

Organization

The poems are offered in two formats: the author's original version and the cloze form. In the cloze form, words have been deleted from the end of several stanzas at regular intervals throughout. When the poem is presented to the students, they are asked to fill in the blanks for the words that have been eliminated. Once the students have completed each cloze selection, they will be able to compare their version of the poem to the author's original. Reinforcement and enrichment suggestions accompany each poem as well.

Rationale

The advantage of presenting passages to students in the cloze format is many-fold. As the students insert the deleted words, they are compelled to construct meaning from the text. Comprehension, critical thinking and vocabulary are reinforced as contextual clues are analyzed: synonyms, antonyms, signal words, and pronoun referents name a few. A wide range of skills and understandings can also be assessed, including the features of language, such as grammar, the identification and use of context clues, and grasp of spelling patterns. Presenting poetry to children in a cloze format has an additional advantage. Students gain valuable practice in the components of phonemic awareness, which is an important step in the reading process. Extending the poems in such areas as rhyming, alliteration, segmentation, and phoneme isolation are all a natural result.

As each poem is read, the students are actively involved. As they progress through the accompanying activities, they are taken to a higher level of thinking: connecting, predicting, summarizing, concluding, questioning, monitoring, evaluating, and applying the information to which they have been exposed.

Before Reading

It is recommended that the pre-reading activities be conducted first. During this phase, a purpose and a plan for reading is established. The activities presented are designed specifically to spark the students' interest. While accessing their background knowledge, these activities help prepare the students to read as active participants. At the same time, the teacher is given an opportunity to evaluate the level of the students' knowledge on the topic. The pre-reading activities also promote the students' engagement and interest by providing them with a means to anticipate the text. Such preparatory activity is critical for comprehension to occur.

Teaching Strategies

The Cloze Activity

Once the pre-reading activities are complete, the students are ready to participate in the structured cloze activity. During reading, they will be connecting their background knowledge and purpose for reading to the text. A step-by-step example of a teacher-directed cloze lesson follows. As the students become familiar with the process, it can become a more independent activity.

First reading: The students are instructed to listen, and depending on their grade and/or instructional levels, asked to point to the words as the teacher reads the entire poem orally, modeling appropriate expression, intonation, and phrasing. The word "blank" is read for each blank space. The students are instructed to think about what would fit in the blanks as they listen to the poem. No pencils are used at this point.

Second reading: The students are instructed to listen a second time to the poem. This time the teacher pauses as the students fill in the blank spaces.

Third reading: As the teacher reads the poem a third time, the students are given the opportunity to volunteer the words they have chosen. As the word choices are written on the board or overhead, discussion evolves, covering the appropriateness of each choice as it relates to the context of the text, the rhyme at the end of each stanza, etc. (For future reading, it is important that all class members have the same choice in each blank. Therefore, the class must come to a consensus as to which word fits best.)

Fourth reading: Each student is given a highlighter to use. As the teacher reads the poem this time, students are asked to highlight the rhyming words at the end of each stanza. (This needs to be a structured teacher-directed activity at first. Students will soon get the idea and be able to do this part independently.)

Choral Reading: Having heard the poem several times, the students are now ready for the "During Reading" activity. Repeated readings help to build the reader's fluency, with improved comprehension as an end result. Comparing the word choices they have made to the author's is a motivating factor at this point. The students should keep their poems together in a folder or file, so that they can be read and re-read frequently.

After Reading

A series of guided reading questions and activities are offered in the after-reading phase. Through discussion and active participation, the readers are able to make connections between their prior knowledge and the information they have learned. At this time, the teacher has one more opportunity to assess comprehension and understanding. Reading support activities are included in this phase as well, offering additional practice in recognizing the sounds on which our language is based, an important step in the reading process. There are also many opportunities to develop reading fluency, through choral, paired, and repeated reading activities.

Animals and Feathered Friends

As Soon As It's Fall

Aileen Fisher

Rabbits and foxes as soon as it's fall
Get coats that are warm with no trouble at all.
Coats that are furry and woolly and new,
Heavy and thick so the cold can't get through.

They don't have to buy them
Or dye them or try them,
They don't have to knit them
Or weave them or fit them,

They don't have to sew them
Or stitch them all through,
They just have to grow them,
And that's what they do.

"As Soon as It's Fall" from CRICKET IN A THICKET by Aileen
Fisher. Copyright 1969 by Thomas Y Crowell. Used by permission
of Marian Reiner for the Boulder Public Library Foundation.

As Soon As It's Fall

Objectives

- Students will explain the main idea the author suggests.

Materials

- cloze copy of the poem (page 8)
- highlighter and pencil for each student
- chart paper
- board or overhead space for a Venn diagram

Before Reading

1. Discuss the different ways animals stay warm in winter. How is it different for us?
2. Using a Venn diagram (See "Mother's Little Girl" on page 103 for an example), and with student input, chart words that describe the similarities and differences between animal coats and the coats we wear. You might want to include in the discussion how the coats are made, how they look, how they feel, where they come from, etc.
3. As they read the poem, have students listen for additional details to add to the Venn diagram.

During Reading

1. Divide the class into three groups, by rows or by counting off, for example.
2. Conduct a choral reading activity as follows: Reading orally with the teacher, group one reads stanza one, group two reads stanza two, group three reads stanza three. (The groups that are not reading follow along.)
3. Switch groups and stanzas so that each group has a chance to practice each stanza at least once.
4. End with a choral reading of the entire poem by the whole group. Encourage good expression, phrasing, and intonation.

After Reading

1. Ask students to highlight the details in the poem that describe animal coats. Discuss, adding details to the Venn diagram above.
2. What is the main idea the author suggests? (*Animals are lucky. They grow their coats with no trouble at all, while we have to go through so much trouble to make one!*)
3. Write the following question words on the board or overhead: *who, what, where, why, when,* and *how.*
4. Ask the students to copy these words on paper and compose a question that can be answered from the poem beginning with each one.
5. Call on volunteers to ask a classmate a question they have written. Continue until most of the details from the poem have been covered.

Reading Support

- Have students go back and circle words in the poem that contain the *th–* sound. Brainstorm on the board or overhead, other words they know that begin with this sound.

As Soon As It's Fall

Aileen Fisher

Rabbits and foxes as soon as it's <u>fall</u>

Get coats that are warm with no trouble at _____

Coats that are furry and woolly and <u>new</u>,

Heavy and thick so the cold can't get _____.

They don't have to buy them

Or dye them or try <u>them</u>,

They don't have to knit them

Or weave them or fit _____,

They don't have to sew them

Or stitch them all <u>through</u>,

They just have to grow them,

And that's what they _____ .

As Soon As It's Fall

Directions: The following story has been started for you. Using details from the poem and the Venn diagram, write a few sentences to complete the story. Choose your own title, then share your story with the class.

_____

(title)

Animals are lucky! They grow their coats with no trouble

at all. _____

_____

_____

_____

_____

_____

_____

_____

Bluebird

Aileen Fisher

In the woods a piece of sky

fell down, a piece of blue.

"It must have come from very high,"

I said. "It looks so new."

It landed on a leafy tree

and there it seemed to cling,

and when I squinted up to see,

I saw it had a *wing*,

And then a *head*, and suddenly

I heard a bluebird sing!

Bluebird

Objectives

- Using details from the poem, students will guess the title and infer whom it is about.

Materials

- a cloze copy of the poem (page 12)
- a highlighter
- sheet of heavy paper and a pencil for each student
- *Chicken Little* by Sally Hobson (New York: Simon & Schuster Books for Young Readers, 1994) or any retelling of the folktale

Before Reading

1. Ask students what they remember about the folktale *Chicken Little*.
2. Read Sally Hobson's, or any other retelling of the folktale, to them.
3. For discussion: What made Chicken Little think the sky was falling? Why do you think the fox lured Chicken Little and her friends into his cave? What other reasons could he have had for doing this?
4. Have students write a title of their own for the poem.
5. Discuss and log their choices on the board.

During Reading

1. Have students cover all stanzas. Then read the poem to the students, one line at a time. They should uncover each line only as it is read. Pause at the end of each line for students to guess whom they think the poem is about.
2. Have them highlight the clues that support their answer. Emphasize how the guesses change as additional clues are discovered.

After Reading

1. Compare the students' title choices to the author's title. How many titles are the same as the author's? How many titles are different? Are all of them appropriate? Why or why not?
2. Continue the discussion: How are the book and the poem the same? How are they different? Can you think of anything else that might fall from the sky to make someone think the sky was falling? Have you ever observed or experienced anything that seemed different than it really was? What was it? How did you figure it out?

Reading Support

- Highlight words in the poem that have the *–ed* ending. What are the base words for each? Think of a new sentence for each base word.
- Copy the poem on the board or overhead. Draw a slash mark between the phrases of each line (e.g., In the woods / a piece of sky). Read each line of the poem with the students slowly, pointing to the words and pausing between phrases. Continue until all lines have been read. Repeat a second time, then go back to the actual poem and read chorally together. Repeat from the beginning, if necessary.

Bluebird

Aileen Fisher

In the woods a piece of <u>sky</u>

fell down, a piece of blue.

"It must have come from very _____,"

I said. "It looks so new."

It landed on a leafy tree

and there it seemed to <u>cling</u>,

and when I squinted up to see,

I saw it had a *wing*,

and then a *head*, and suddenly

I heard a bluebird _____!

Bluebird

Directions: Review the five parts of a friendly letter:

- *Heading:* Consists of the street address on the first line; the city, state and zip code on the second line; the date on the third line
- *Greeting:* Dear . . . ,
- *Body:* The main text or message
- *Closing:* It means good-bye—Sincerely, Your friend, etc.
- *Signature:* Tells who wrote the letter

Using this friendly letter format, pretend to write a letter to the author. In your letter, explain to her how you feel about her poem. Then explain some ways that "Bluebird" and *Chicken Little* are the same.

_____

_____

_____

_____,

_____

_____

_____

_____

_____,

_____

The Hairy Dog

Herbert Asquith

My dog's so furry I've not seen

His face for years and years:

His eyes are buried out of sight,

I only guess his ears.

When people ask me for his breed,

I do not know or care:

He has the beauty of them all

Hidden beneath his hair.

The Hairy Dog

Objectives

- Students will compare and contrast the dog in Herbert Asquith's poem with other dogs they know.

Materials

- a copy of the cloze form of the poem (page 16)
- a highlighter and pencil for each student
- large chart paper or overhead
- a copy of the book *Puppies*, by Carrie Scott (DK Publishing, Inc. 1997) or any book or article that illustrates breeds of dogs

Before Reading

1. Poll the class as to how many own dogs of their own.
2. Chart on the board, chart paper, or overhead, the different kinds (breeds) of dogs they suggest. For each breed, add additional details. (For example: size, type of hair, and color)
3. Save chart for future reference.
4. Search for illustrations of the dogs they mentioned in the book *Puppies* by Carrie Scott (or use any book or article that illustrates different kinds of dogs).
5. Tell students to be ready to tell if the description of the dog in the poem matches any of the dogs in the chart.

During Reading

1. Model good fluency by reading "The Hairy Dog" out loud to the students.
2. Discuss with the students what they liked about the way you read the poem.
3. Lead the choral reading, softening your voice as their fluency improves.

After Reading

1. Highlight the details in the poem that describe Herbert Asquith's dog. Do the details for the dog in the poem match any in the chart? What details are the same? What details are different?
2. Make an entry in the chart for Herbert Asquith's dog. What breed of dog do you think this could be? Look at the book illustrations for help.
3. Use the following question as a point of discussion: What does the author mean when he says the dog "has the beauty of them all hidden beneath his hair"? (*His dog has the best qualities of all the breeds put together.*)

Reading Support

- Divide the class into three or four groups. Assign one of the rhyming patterns to each group. Have each group create a word list for their phoneme. Then combine into a class chart that can be displayed and re-read periodically.

The Hairy Dog
Herbert Asquith

My dog's so furry I've not seen

His face for years and <u>years</u>:

His eyes are buried out of sight,

I only guess his _____ .

When people ask me for his breed,

I do not know or <u>care</u>:

He has the beauty of them all

Hidden beneath his _____ .

The Hairy Dog

Directions: Choose one of the dogs from the chart created earlier. Then complete the sentences below, using details from the poem or from the chart to help you.

Herbert Asquith's dog and a _____ dog are

the same because_____

_____

_____.

They are different because _____

_____

_____

_____.

I like a _____ dog best because _____

_____

_____.

Little Joey

Helen Kitchell Evans

Nature gave the kangaroo
A most convenient pocket
And little Joey rides inside
Like a picture in a pocket.

Mamma kangaroo just leaps
When she goes anywhere
But little Joey thinks it's fun
To go sailing in the air.

When Joey gets scared while at play
He races like a rocket.
Toward the mamma kangaroo
And jumps back in her pocket.

"Little Joey" by Helen Kitchell Evans. From POETRY PLACE
ANTHOLOGY. Copyright© 1983 by Edgell Communications Inc.
Reprinted by permission of Scholastic Inc.

Little Joey

Objectives

- Students will recognize the sequence of the story by rearranging the lines of the stanzas in correct order.

Materials

- cloze copy of the poem (page 20)
- a highlighter and a pencil for each student
- overhead or board space
- sentence strips with the title and each line of the poem written on them
- pocket chart or board space suitable for rearranging the sentence strips

Before Reading

1. Put the following words from the poem on the board or overhead: *nature, convenient, pocket, rides, leaps,* and *jumps.*
2. Pronounce and discuss each word. Knowing that these are actual words from the poem, ask students to think of different topics the poem might be about. List the topics on the board or overhead. (If the topic does not come up, add other words from the poem until *kangaroos* is guessed.)
3. Brainstorm and web student knowledge of kangaroos. Include basic characteristics and unique features in the discussion (kangaroos are mammals, the babies are born alive and are carried in their mother's pouch, a baby kangaroo is called a Joey, kangaroos move quickly by hopping on their strong hind legs, they use their tails to prop themselves up, etc.).

During Reading

1. The teacher reads the first line of the poem, modeling good expression and phrasing, as the students follow along.
2. The students then echo back the first line, following along with their fingers. Continue in the same manner until all lines have been read. Repeat as needed.
3. Conclude with a choral reading of the entire poem by the whole class.

After Reading

- Call off the vocabulary words mentioned above and have students highlight them in the poem.
- For discussion, ask the following questions: To what does the author compare the kangaroo's pouch? Is this a good comparison? Why or why not? To what else could we compare the pouch? What makes mamma's "pocket" so convenient for little Joey? What useful purpose do our pockets serve?

Reading Support

Have the class close their books or put the poem away. Divide the class into pairs. Give one prewritten sentence strip to each pair. The teacher reads the title of the poem. The students with that sentence strip place it in the top of the pocket chart. The teacher reads the first line of the poem. The students with that sentence strip place it under the title. Ask, "What did nature give the kangaroo?" The student with the line that answers that question places it under the last one. Continue in the same manner until all sentence strips are in place, in the correct order. Offer clues only when needed. Then have the group read the poem together from the sentence strips.

Little Joey

Helen Kitchell Evans

Nature gave the kangaroo

A most convenient <u>pocket</u>

And little Joey rides inside

Like a picture in a _____ .

Mamma kangaroo just leaps

When she goes <u>anywhere</u>

But little Joey thinks it's fun

To go sailing in the _____ .

When Joey gets scared while at play

He races like a <u>rocket</u>.

Toward the mamma kangaroo

And jumps back in her _____ .

Little Joey

Directions: Complete the sentences below comparing yourself (when you were little) to Little Joey. Illustrate on the back of the paper if time permits.

Little Joey goes for rides in his mother's _____.

This is fun for him because _____

_____

_____.

When I was little, my mother took me for rides in _____.

This was fun for me because _____

_____

_____.

When he is scared, Little Joey _____

_____

_____

_____.

When I was little and I was scared, I _____

_____

_____

_____.

Little Turtle

Vachel Lindsay

There was a little turtle.
He lived in a box.
He swam in a puddle.
He climbed on the rocks.

He snapped at a mosquito.
He snapped at a flea.
He snapped at a minnow.
And he snapped at me.

He caught the mosquito.
He caught the flea.
He caught the minnow.
But he didn't catch me.

Little Turtle

Objectives

- After reading a poem and a non-fiction book, students will identify whether a series of statements are true or false.

Materials

- a cloze copy of the poem (page 24)
- a highlighter and a pencil for each student
- *All About Turtles*, by Jim Arnosky, (Scholastic Press, NY, 2000), or any other non-fiction book on turtles.
- overhead or board space

Before Reading

- The students should complete the activity page before any reading or discussion takes place, indicating from their background knowledge, whether they consider the statements true or false.
- A discussion on turtles should follow. Write a few headings on the board or overhead: Where Turtles Live, What Turtles Eat, What Turtles Look Like, What Turtles Do, etc.
- Using student input, list their responses.
- Read *All About Turtles*, or any other non-fiction book on turtles, to the class. Verify details given; add new information to the chart above. Save.
- Tell students to look for factual information they can add to the chart as they read the poem.

During Reading

1. Divide the class into three groups.
2. Assign each group one stanza of the poem.
3. One student within each group becomes the narrator, while the others act out the story. Reunite the group.
4. Ask them to read and act out the stanzas in order.

After Reading

- Students highlight information in the poem that is factual. Verify and discuss. "According to the poem, what do turtles eat? Where do they live? What do they do?" Add new information to the chart.
- Turn to the activity page once again. Have the students re-read the statements, changing their true and false answers when needed. Come to a consensus as to which statements are true and which are false. Ask them to change words in the false statements to make them true. Verify.

Reading Support

Divide the class into three groups. Assign each group one stanza of the poem. Have the groups practice reading their stanza chorally, until they are ready to perform before the group. Reconvene. While the first group is reading the first stanza, the second group acts it out. While the second group reads the second stanza, the third group acts it out. While the third group reads the third stanza, the first group acts it out. Conclude by reading the entire poem chorally together, with everyone acting it out.

Answers for page 25: 1. Yes 2. No 3. Yes 4. No 5. Yes 6. Yes 7. No 8. Yes 9. No 10. No

Little Turtle
Vachel Lindsay

There was a little turtle.

He lived in a <u>box</u>.

He swam in a puddle.

He climbed on the _____ .

He snapped at a mosquito.

He snapped at a <u>flea</u>.

He snapped at a minnow.

And he snapped at _____ .

He caught the mosquito.

He caught the <u>flea</u>.

He caught the minnow.

But he didn't catch _____ .

Little Turtle

Directions: Before reading, read or listen to the following statements below. On the line in front of each statement, write *yes* if you think the statement is true. Write *no* if you think it is not true.

Then after reading, read the statements again. Are there any you want to change? Correct the false statements to make them true.

_____**1.** Turtles are reptiles.

_____**2.** No matter what the temperature, turtles always stay warm.

_____**3.** Turtles hibernate in winter.

_____**4.** Turtle shells are made of plastic.

_____**5.** Sea turtles do not live in their shells.

_____**6.** Turtles have excellent eyesight.

_____**7.** Turtles do not have a good sense of smell.

_____**8.** Turtles have a good sense of touch.

_____**9.** Turtles eat only plants.

_____**10.** Turtle babies are born alive.

The Snow-Bird

Frank Dempster Sherman

When all the ground with snow is white
The merry snow-bird comes,
And hops about with great delight
To find the scattered crumbs.

How glad he seems to get to eat
A piece of cake or bread!
He wears no shoes upon his feet,
nor hat upon his head.

But happiest is he, I know,
Because no cage with bars
Keeps him from walking on the snow
And printing it with stars.

The Snow-Bird

Objectives

- Students will determine the main idea of the poem.

Materials

- a cloze copy of the poem (page 28)
- a highlighter and a pencil for each student

Before Reading

- Open with a discussion on the change of seasons, particularly the change from fall to winter. What stays the same during each season? What changes? What adjustments do people make when winter comes? What adjustments do wild animals make? Birds? (*Some migrate and fly south while others stay in the north.*) How do birds that stay north survive? (*They grow thicker coats, just like dogs and cats do.*) What kind of food is available for them? (*They change from a diet of live bugs to a menu of seeds, berries, and hibernating insects.*) Where do they find their food? How can we help the birds that stay north? Name some birds you have seen here in the winter.

During Reading

1. While reading the poem, have students think about the main idea the author suggests.
2. Then review the concept that synonyms are words with similar meanings. Give a few examples. Ask the students to write a synonym above each of the following words in the poem: *merry, hops, find, glad, happiest, walking,* and *printing.* Verify. Re-read the poem, using the synonyms instead of the original words. Does the poem still make sense?

After Reading

- For discussion: Where does this story take place? What is a Snow-Bird? How do you know the Snow-Birds in the poem are happy? Highlight the details that show this. What is the main idea the author is suggesting? (*The main reason the birds are happy is because they are free.*) What does the author mean when he says the birds print the snow with stars?

Reading Support

After the initial lesson, reread the poem chorally several times over the course of the day. At the end of the day, after the last choral reading, ask for individual volunteers to read the poem to the class by themselves.

The Snow-Bird

Frank Dempster Sherman

When all the ground with snow is white

The merry snow-bird <u>comes</u>,

And hops about with great delight

To find the scattered _____ .

How glad he seems to get to eat

A piece of cake or <u>bread</u>!

He wears no shoes upon his feet,

nor hat upon his _____ .

But happiest is he, I know,

Because no cage with <u>bars</u>

Keeps him from walking on the snow

And printing it with _____ .

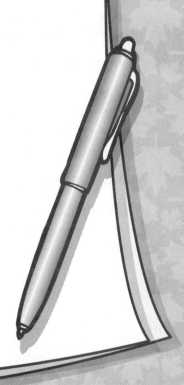

The Snow-Bird

Directions: Fill in the chart below, comparing the life of birds living in a cage to those that are free.

BIRDS IN A CAGE

BIRDS THAT ARE FREE

Birds in a cage are happy when . . .	Birds that are free are happy when . . .
Birds in a cage are not happy when . . .	Birds that are free are not happy when . . .
Birds in a cage are in danger when . . .	Birds that are free are in danger when . . .

Woodpecker

Elizabeth Madox Roberts

The woodpecker pecked out
A little round hole
And made him a house
In a telephone pole.

One day when I watched
He poked out his head
And had on a hood
And a collar of red.

When the streams of rain
Pour out of the sky,
And the sparkles of lightning
Go flashing by,

And the big, big wheels
Of thunder roll,
He can snuggle back in
The telephone pole.

Woodpecker

Objectives

- Students will extract details from the text indicating what they have learned about woodpeckers.

Materials

- a copy of Katherine Grier's book *Downy Woodpecker* (Grolier, Connecticut, 1986) or any other non-fiction book or article with information on woodpeckers
- a highlighter and a pencil for each student
- a cloze copy of the poem (page 32)
- a photocopy (or have the students copy) of a KWL chart for each student labeled as follows:

WOODPECKERS

I Know	I Wonder	I Learned

Before Reading

1. Let the students know that the poem they are going to read is about woodpeckers.
2. Have them copy, or hand out copies of, the KWL Chart. Ask the students to fill in the first column with facts they already know. In the second column, tell them to jot down what they would like to know or what they wonder about woodpeckers. Review the questions they have written.
3. Have the students read the poem to see if any of their questions are answered.

During Reading

1. *First reading:* Modeling good fluency, the teacher reads the entire poem to the class, as the students follow along.
2. *Second reading:* The teacher reads the first line, the students chorally read the second line with him or her, the teacher reads the third line, the students read the fourth line with him or her, etc. Continue alternating until the whole poem has been read.
3. *Third reading:* The students read the first line, the teacher reads the second line, etc. Continue alternating until the whole poem has been read a second time.
4. *Fourth reading:* Teacher and students read the entire poem chorally together.

After Reading

- For discussion, ask the following questions: Were any of your questions answered? Which ones?
- Highlight details in the poem that show where the woodpecker lives and what the woodpecker looks like. Add this information to the What I Learned column in your chart. How did the woodpecker feel during the thunderstorm? How do you know?
- Ask students to respond to the following questions (You may want to log responses for later verification.): "Where else do you think woodpeckers live?" "What do think they might eat?" "Can you describe a woodpecker's bill?" "How is its tongue designed to help it catch food?" "How many eggs does the female lay?" "How long before the eggs hatch?" "How long before the babies can look out for themselves?" Students listen to *Downy Woodpecker* by Katherine Grier (or any non-fiction book or article on woodpeckers) to verify their answers to these questions, and for other information to add to the What I Learned column in the chart.

Reading Support

Ask students to highlight the long vowel words in the poem. Chart by spelling patterns (*–ole, –oke, –eam, –ain, –y, –ight,* and *–eel*). List student responses as they offer additional words in each category.

Woodpecker

Elizabeth Madox Roberts

The woodpecker pecked out

a little round <u>hole</u>

And made him a house

in a telephone _____ .

One day when I watched

he poked out his <u>head</u>

And had on a hood

and a collar of _____ .

When the streams of rain

pour out of the <u>sky</u>,

And the sparkles of lightning

go flashing _____ ,

And the big, big wheels

of thunder <u>roll</u>,

He can snuggle back in

the telephone _____ .

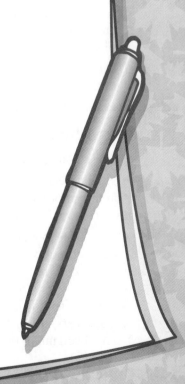

Woodpecker

Directions: Using your KWL Chart for information, think of some questions to ask your classmates about woodpeckers. Use the question words below as a start. Remember, the answers must come from the KWL chart. Then take turns playing the teacher game. Ask your teacher to play too! (See page 105 for directions.)

Who . . .

What . . .

Where . . .

Why . . .

When . . .

How . . .

Fun

and

Play

The Balloon Man

Rose Fyleman

He always comes on market days,
    And holds balloons—a lovely bunch—
And in the market square he stays,
    And never seems to think of lunch.

They're red and purple, blue and green,
    And when it is a sunny day
Tho' carts and people get between
    You see them shining far away.

And some are big and some are small,
    All tied together with a string,
And if there is a wind at all
    They tug and tug like anything.

Some day perhaps he'll let them go
    And we shall see them sailing high,
And stand and watch them from below—
    They *would* look pretty in the sky!

The Balloon Man

Objectives

- Using details from the poem, students will determine its setting: the time (past, present, or future) and the place in which it occurs.

Materials

- a cloze copy of the poem (page 37)
- a highlighter and a pencil for each student
- chart paper
- overhead or board space

Before Reading

1. Write the title of the poem on the board. From the title, ask the students to predict about what they think the poem is going to be. Lead them to discuss questions such as the following: What is a balloon man? What does he do? Where might you find one? How would you know he was there?

2. Remind students that the setting of a story or poem is the time (when) and place where it occurs. Understanding the setting of a story is important because it not only establishes the mood of the story, but also helps the reader visualize the events that are taking place. Model the setting of a familiar story or poem, like "Hiding" on page 43, for example. When did "Hiding" take place: in the past, present, or future? How do you know? Where did the story take place? What details in the poem might change if it took place in a different time?

3. Tell students that after reading "The Balloon Man," they will be asked to describe where and when it took place.

During Reading

1. Explain paired reading to the class (two readers practice reading a section of text together). Using a student volunteer, model paired reading for the class. Demonstrate adjusting the pace and volume to provide the maximum effect.

2. Divide the class into pairs, putting an early reader with a more fluent reader whenever possible. Allow the pairs to practice reading and rereading the poem several times.

3. End with a choral class reading of the entire poem.

After Reading

- Discuss the setting of the poem. Does it take place in the past, present, or future? What makes you think so? Where does the poem take place? Highlight details to prove this.

- Ask students the following questions: According to the author, what is a balloon man? What does he do? Where does the narrator find him? How does she know he is there? What does she want him to do? Why does she want him to do this? Do you think he will do it? Why or why not? Can you think of places we would find a balloon man today? What details in the poem would change if the setting changed to one of these places? What different kinds of balloons are familiar to you?

Reading Support

Choose six rhyming pairs from the poem to write on the board or overhead. Using student input, add other words that rhyme with each pair.

The Balloon Man

Rose Fyleman

He always comes on market days,

   And holds balloons—a lovely <u>bunch</u>—

And in the market square he stays,

   And never seems to think of _____.

They're red and purple, blue and green,

   And when it is a sunny <u>day</u>

Tho' carts and people get between

   You see them shining far _____.

And some are big and some are small,

   All tied together with a <u>string</u>,

And if there is a wind at all

   They tug and tug like any _____.

Some day perhaps he'll let them go

   And we shall see them sailing <u>high</u>,

And stand and watch them from below—

   They *would* look pretty in the _____ !

The Balloon Man

Directions: Write a rhyming pair from the poem in each balloon. Then draw the balloon man in the empty space.

A Good Play

Robert Louis Stevenson

We built a ship upon the stairs
All made of the back-bedroom chairs,
And filled it full of sofa pillows
To go a-sailing on the billows.

We took a saw and several nails,
And water in the nursery pails;
And Tom said, "Let us also take
An apple and a slice of cake;"—
Which was enough for Tom and me
To go a-sailing on, till tea.

We sailed along for days and days
And had the very best of plays;
But Tom fell out and hurt his knee,
So there was no one left but me.

A Good Play

Objectives

- Students will (a) identify the characters in the poem, the setting, and the main events; and (b) predict what happens next.

Materials

- a cloze copy of the poem (page 41)
- a highlighter and a pencil for each student

Before Reading

1. Discuss activities that kids like to do inside. (*Television, video games, and computers are sure to be mentioned.*) Are there any board games they like to play?

2. Have them think of some pretend games they like that require their imaginations (pirates, army, house, dolls, etc.). Where do the ideas come from for these games of imagination? (*books, movies, television*)

3. Ask the students to pretend they are playing inside and have decided to "go sailing." Where in the house would they "build" their ship? With what would they use to "build" it? List the items mentioned on the board. What are some adventures they might have as they "sail" on the seas? What items would they need to take on the ship in order to act out these adventures? Add these items to the list as well.

During Reading

1. Divide the class into seven groups, one group for each stanza of the poem.

2. Have each group practice reading its stanza chorally several times.

3. When they have become proficient, have them decide how they want to act it out. (They may add props at your discretion)

4. Finally, have each group present its stanza to the group.

After Reading

- For discussion, ask the following questions: Where does the story in the poem take place? When does it take place: in the past, the present, or the future? How do you know?

- Compare Robert Louis Stevenson's ideas to the ideas you had. Where did the kids in the poem build their ship? What did they use to build it?

- According to the poem, what are *billows*? (*waves*) Highlight everything in the poem the "sailors" took with them. Did you take the same things? Different things? How long did the narrator say their trip lasted? Could this be true? Why or why not? What happened to Tom? How do you think he fell out? What do you think might happen next in the story?

Reading Support

Pick a word from the poem that can be easily rhymed, such as the word *ship*. Say, "Ship, hip—*ship* rhymes with *hip*." Have the students repeat this chant with you and write the words down. Say, "Stairs, hairs—*stairs* rhymes with *hairs*." Students repeat with you and record it on paper. Now call on student volunteers to pick other words from the poem and make up rhyming chants similar to these and record them on paper.

A Good Play

Robert Louis Stevenson

We built a ship upon the <u>stairs</u>

All made of the back-bedroom _____,

And filled it full of sofa pillows

To go a-sailing on the billows.

We took a saw and several <u>nails</u>,

And water in the nursery _____;

And Tom said, "Let us also take

An apple and a slice of cake;"—

Which was enough for Tom and <u>me</u>

To go a-sailing on, till _____.

We sailed along for days and days

And had the very best of plays;

But Tom fell out and hurt his <u>knee</u>,

So there was no one left but _____.

A Good Play

Directions: Write a few sentences to complete the story map below.

> WHO are the main characters in the poem?

> WHERE does the story take place?

> WHEN does the story take place?

> WHAT are the main events that happen in the story?

> HOW do you think the story continues?
> (What do you think happens next?)

Hiding

Dorothy Aldis

I'm hiding, I'm hiding,
And no one knows where;
For all they can see is my
Toes and my hair.

And I just heard my father
Say to my mother—
"But, darling, he must be
Somewhere or other;

Have you looked in the inkwell?"
And mother said, "Where?"
"In the inkwell," said Father. But
I was not there.

Then "Wait!" cried my Mother—
"I think that I see
Him under the carpet." But
It was not me.

"Inside the mirror's
A pretty good place,"
Said Father and looked, but saw
Only his face.

"We've hunted," sighed Mother,
"As hard as we could
And I am so afraid that we've
Lost him for good."

Then I laughed out aloud
And I wiggled my toes
And Father said—"Look, dear,
I wonder if those

Toes could be Benny's.
There are ten of them. See?"
And they were surprised to find
Out it was me!

Hiding

Objectives

- Students will construct a story map identifying the title, characters, problem, and solution.

Materials

- a copy of the cloze version of the poem (page 45)
- a colored highlighter for each student
- pencil for the writing and illustrating tasks

Before Reading

1. In order to model the objective stated above, choose a fairy tale or story with which the students are familiar such as "Cinderella." With help from the students, outline on the board the title, characters, problem, and solution for this story. Save the outline so that students may refer back to it during the after-reading activities.
2. Then discuss the game Hide-and-Seek. What are the rules of the game? Where is the game usually played? Brainstorm good hiding places, both inside and out.
3. Tell the students that after "Hiding" is read, they may be asked to identify the characters and explain the problem and solution.

During Reading

1. Divide the class into four groups.
2. Assign two stanzas of the poem to each group.
3. Have the groups practice their stanzas chorally together, encouraging good expression, phrasing, and intonation.
4. Choose a student volunteer to become the actor. As the groups read the stanzas in sequence, the actor acts it out.
5. Reread several times, choosing other volunteers to assume the role of the actor.

After Reading

- Divide the class into small groups. Give them some time to discuss the characters in the poem, the problem, and how it is solved. Reconvene. Through whole group discussion and agreement, create a class chart indicating the story elements discussed: Title, Characters, Problem, and Solution.
- For discussion, ask the following questions: Where did Mother and Father look for Benny? What made each of these places unlikely ones for him to be? In what time period do you think this poem takes place? How do you know? What are the two main clues as to Benny's whereabouts? Where do you think Benny is hiding? Highlight the details in the poem that give you this idea. What are some reasons Benny may have been hiding from his parents?

Reading Support

Have the students highlight words in the poem that contain a short vowel sound. Give them a time limit in which to accomplish this task. Categorize on the board. Are all the vowel sounds represented?

Hiding
Dorothy Aldis

I'm hiding, I'm hiding,

And no one knows <u>where</u>;

For all they can see is my

Toes and my _____.

And I just heard my father

Say to my <u>mother</u>—

"But, darling, he must be

Somewhere or _____;

Have you looked in the inkwell?"

And mother said, "<u>Where</u>?"

"In the inkwell," said Father. But

I was not _____.

Then "Wait!" cried my Mother—

"I think that I <u>see</u>

Him under the carpet." But

It was not _____.

"Inside the mirror's

A pretty good <u>place</u>,"

Said Father and looked, but saw

Only his _____.

"We've hunted," sighed Mother,

"As hard as we <u>could</u>

And I am so afraid that we've

Lost him for _____."

Then I laughed out aloud

And I wiggled my <u>toes</u>

And Father said—"Look, dear,

I wonder if _____

Toes could be Benny's.

There are ten of them. <u>See</u>?"

And they were surprised to find

Out it was _____!

Hiding

Directions: In the poem "Hiding," the author does not tell us where Benny is hiding or why he is there. However, we can guess from the details in the poem where he might be. In the space below, draw an illustration to show where you think Benny is hiding. Use details from the poem to help you. Then, in a few sentences underneath your picture, explain why you think Benny is hiding there.

The Lost Balloon

Marion Parker

Oh, I had a balloon.

It was round, it was red.

Such a lovely balloon,

Almost as big as my head.

But I heard a loud noise,

And I looked around to see

For I wondered just what

Made that loud noise at me.

And then when I looked

My balloon was not there!

It was not on the floor,

It was not on the chair.

I've looked and I've looked,

But it's not to be found.

Have you seen my balloon?

It was red, it was round.

"The Lost Balloon" by Marion Parker. From POETRY PLACE
ANTHOLOGY. Copyright© 1983 by Edgell Communications Inc.
Reprinted by permission of Scholastic Inc.

The Lost Balloon

Objectives

- Students will (a) distinguish the cause effect relationships developed in the poem, and (b) predict what happens next.

Materials

- a cloze copy of the poem (page 49)
- a highlighter and a pencil for each student
- chart paper
- overhead or board space
- paper for the writing activity

Before Reading

1. Write the word *balloon* on the chalkboard or overhead.
2. Ask students to offer ways a child might "lose" a balloon. Chart these responses in a web format and save.
3. Tell the students that in "The Lost Balloon," there is a loud noise. Ask them to be thinking about what might have caused it.

During Reading

1. While modeling good fluency, read the entire poem to the class as the students follow along.
2. Then conduct a whole group choral reading of the poem. During a second choral reading, the first student in the first row will be the starter. He or she will read the first line. The student behind him or her will join him or her on the second line, the next student will join them on the third line, etc., until eventually all classmates are reading.
3. Repeat as many times as you wish, choosing different students in different rows to begin.

After Reading

- For discussion, ask the following:
  1. Where does this story take place? Highlight details that prove this.
  2. What is the loud noise? Highlight details that make you think this is true. (Elicit that the "loud noise" was the balloon popping.) Go back to the web above. Circle ways a child might lose a balloon that would apply in this case. What else could have caused the balloon to pop?
  3. Where does the child look for the balloon? Does he or she realize the balloon has popped? Circle details that prove this to be true.
  4. To whom do you think the narrator of the poem is talking? What makes you think so?
- Ask students to underline words in the poem that describe the balloon.
- Have students write one or two sentences on scrap paper to continue the story. Share and discuss as to relevancy as time permits.

Reading Support

Have students circle words in the poem that contain the *–ou* phoneme. List other words they think of that contain this phoneme.

The Lost Balloon
Marion Parker

Oh, I had a balloon.

It was round, it was <u>red</u>.

Such a lovely balloon,

Almost as big as my _____.

But I heard a loud noise,

And I looked around to <u>see</u>

For I wondered just what

Made that loud noise at _____.

And then when I looked

My balloon was not <u>there</u>!

It was not on the floor,

It was not on the _____.

I've looked and I've looked,

But it's not to be <u>found</u>.

Have you seen my balloon?

It was red, it was _____.

The Lost Balloon

Directions: Pretend you are the child in the poem. Draw an illustration to show how you think the balloon popped. In your illustration, include as many details from the poem as you can. Then write a title and a few sentences to explain what is happening in your picture.

_____

(title)

_____

_____

_____

_____

March Wind

Eleanor Dennis

We made a brand-new kite today,

And soon as we were through

We came out here to fly it,

And the wind just blew and blew.

And now the kite's a tiny speck;

We've used up all the string;

I'd like to go and get some more.

Anne's such a tiny thing

To hold the kite all by herself;

I wouldn't let her try,

For fear I might look back and see

Anne sailing through the sky.

March Wind

Objectives

- Students will draw conclusions from the poem, by predicting what will happen next after each stanza.

Materials

- a cloze copy of the poem (page 53)
- a piece of heavy paper or large book mark for each student
- transparency
- a highlighter
- a pencil
- overhead projector

Before Reading

Brainstorm the following questions with students: Flying kites—how many have done this? What do you need in order to fly a kite? Have you ever made your own kite? How is it done? What are some designs you have seen? In order to fly kites, what conditions are necessary? Is it easy or hard? Where are some good places to fly kites? What are some bad places? What are some problems that might arise? When is a good time of the year to fly kites?

During Reading

1. Read and discuss the title.
2. Have students cover the stanzas. Reveal the stanzas one at time while doing the activities below.

   Stanza 1: Read, and then discuss: Where do the children in the story get their kite? When do they fly it? What is it like outside? Write in the margin what you think will happen next. Share. What details helped you decide?

   Stanza 2: Read and then discuss: Were your predictions correct? How close were you? What actually happens? Discuss the following: What is the tiny speck? All the string is used up. What has happened? What do you think will happen next—write it in the margin. Share. What details help you decide?

   Stanza 3: Read and then discuss: Were your predictions correct? How close were you? What actually happens? Why won't the narrator let Anne try? Why doesn't the narrator go and get some more string? What do you think will happen next in the story? Write your thoughts in the margin. Share. What details help you decide?

After Reading

Make a transparency copy of "March Wind" for the overhead. Read the lines of the poem to the students one at a time. Underline the phrases as you read them on the overhead copy (e.g., We made a brand new kite today.) The students underline their copies. Choose a random phrase and read it to the students. Have the students locate the phrase, then read it with you as you both point to the words. Continue choosing random phrases to locate, until all the phrases have been read. Finally, read the whole selection chorally together.

Reading Support

Have students circle the contractions in the poem. Then write in the two words that stand for each contraction. Then read the poem again using the two words instead of the contraction. Which version sounds better?

March Wind

Eleanor Dennis

We made a brand-new kite today,

And soon as we were <u>through</u>

We came out here to fly it,

And the wind just blew and _____.

And now the kite's a tiny speck;

We've used up all the <u>string</u>;

I'd like to go and get some more.

Anne's such a tiny _____

To hold the kite all by herself;

I wouldn't let her <u>try</u>,

For fear I might look back and see

Anne sailing through the _____.

March Wind

Directions: Draw an illustration to show what you think would have happened if the narrator left Anne to hold the string. Then write a caption to go with your picture.

_____

(caption)

On the Bridge

Kate Greenaway

If I could see a little fish—
That is what I just now wish!
I want to see his great round eyes
Always open in surprise.

I wish a water rat would glide
Slowly to the other side;
Or a dancing spider sit
On the yellow flags a bit.

I think I'll get some stones to throw,
And watch the pretty circles show,
Or shall we sail a flower-boat,
And watch it slowly—slowly float?

That's nice—because you never know
How far away it means to go;
And when tomorrow comes, you see,
It may be in the great wide sea.

On the Bridge

Objectives

• Using information from the text, the students will identify the setting of the story.

Materials

• a cloze copy of the poem (page 57)   • a highlighter and a pencil for each student

• a map of the United States or the area where you live

Before Reading

1. Open a discussion on bridges: What are some different kinds of bridges? Of what are they made? For what are they used?

2. Brainstorm different places where bridges are found (over highways, railroad tracks, rivers, oceans, etc.)

3. Ask the students to close their eyes and pretend they are standing on one of the bridges they mentioned. What can they see? What sounds do they hear?

4. As they read the poem, ask them to be thinking about where the bridge in the poem is located.

During Reading

1. Read the first stanza of the poem aloud to the students.

2. Ask them to listen closely to your phrasing and intonation.

3. Have the students read this stanza back to you, chorally.

4. Ask them to use the same phrasing and intonation you modeled.

5. Repeat as many times as necessary.

6. Continue in the same manner with the remaining stanzas.

7. Conclude with a group choral reading of the entire poem.

After Reading

• For discussion: Where is the bridge in the poem located? (*over a river*) How do you know? (*It flows to the sea.*) What words does the author use to describe the fish, the water rat, and the spider? How do these descriptions help us when we are reading the poem? Does the narrator actually see the fish, the water rat, and the spider? How do you know? Is the narrator alone on the bridge or with someone else? What makes you think so? What would "yellow flags" be? What do you think a "flower-boat" is? What else might the narrator see as she stands on the bridge? What sounds might she hear? How could the narrator's flower-boat end up in the "great wide sea"? (*Most rivers begin as streams high in the mountains and eventually end up emptying into the sea.*)

• Show the students a map of the United States or the area where you live. Point out several rivers, noting their origin and the seas into which they empty.

Reading Support

Have the students circle the following words in the poem: *eyes, slowly, dancing, flags, stones, circles.*
Categorize and list by ending. From what base word does each come? Think of other words to add to the list which have the same endings.

On the Bridge

Kate Greenaway

If I could see a little <u>fish</u>—

That is what I just now _____!

I want to see his great round eyes

Always open in surprise.

I wish a water rat would <u>glide</u>

Slowly to the other _____;

Or a dancing spider sit

On the yellow flags a bit.

I think I'll get some stones to throw,

And watch the pretty circles show,

Or shall we sail a flower-<u>boat</u>,

And watch it slowly—slowly _____?

That's nice-because you never <u>know</u>

How far away it means to _____;

And when tomorrow comes, you see,

It may be in the great wide sea.

On the Bridge

Directions: Pretend the fish, the water rat, and the spider jumped on the flower-boat just before it was launched. In a few sentences, describe an adventure the three might have as they travel down the river towards the sea. Draw an illustration to accompany your story.

Reading Books
Vivian Gouled

I like to read all kinds of books
To entertain myself,
And so I'm glad when I can take
A book down from the shelf.

I like the picture books of planes,
Of flowers, birds, and ships
From which I can imagine that
I'm taking wonder trips.

I like the books with stories in
And also books of rhymes;
I often try to learn a few
And say them lots of times.

I like to read all kinds of books
I find upon the shelf—
Particularly now that I
Can read all by myself!

"Reading Books" by Vivian Gouled. From POETRY PLACE
ANTHOLOGY. Copyright© 1983 by Edgell Communications Inc.
Reprinted by permission of Scholastic Inc.

Reading Books

Objectives

- Students will distinguish the difference between fiction and non-fiction.

Materials

- a cloze copy of the poem (page 61)
- a highlighter and a pencil for each student
- a selection of fiction and non-fiction books from the classroom library
- large chart paper
- overhead or board space

Before Reading

1. Brainstorm the types of books the students like to read. As they are mentioned, and without telling them why, list in two groups on the board or overhead. Lead the students to categorize one list as fiction and the other as nonfiction. Discuss what each represents. (*A fiction book tells an invented story. A nonfiction book relays factual information.*)
2. Randomly pull books from the selection above. Talk about the title and skim the pages together. Discuss whether the books are fiction or nonfiction and the reasons why.
3. The students should listen for the kinds of books the author likes to read, and be ready to tell whether they are fiction or nonfiction.

During Reading

1. Divide the class into pairs, putting early readers with more fluent readers, if possible.
2. Review your expectations for fluency. Some examples are good expression, phrasing, and intonation.
3. Have the pairs practice reading the poem together several times.
4. Get back together as a whole group, and conduct a choral reading of the entire poem.
5. Do another choral reading, this time designating one student to drop out of the reading after the first line is read. Continue having one student drop out after each additional line is read. Only a few students will be left reading by the end of the poem. Those who are not reading must continue following along.
6. Repeat as time permits, choosing a different student to start dropping out each time the poem is read.

After Reading

For discussion: What kinds of books does the author like to read? Highlight details that prove this. Which would be fiction? Which would be nonfiction? How do you know? Why does she like nonfiction books? Why do fiction books appeal to her? Which do you like best and why? What makes her particularly excited about reading? How did you feel when you first learned to read?

Reading Support

Pronounce the following blended sounds: *gl, pl, fl, fr, tr, st.* Have students go back and circle the words in the poem that contain these sounds. Chart additional words they can think of for each blend.

Reading Books
Vivian Gouled

I like to read all kinds of books

To entertain <u>myself</u>,

And so I'm glad when I can take

A book down from the _____.

I like the picture books of planes,

Of flowers, birds, and <u>ships</u>

From which I can imagine that

I'm taking wonder _____.

I like the books with stories in

And also books of <u>rhymes</u>;

I often try to learn a few

And say them lots of _____.

I like to read all kinds of books

I find upon the <u>shelf</u>—

Particularly now that I

Can read all by _____!

Reading Books

Directions: Draw a cover design for your favorite book. Then in a few sentences, tell what the book is about and why you like it so much.

_____

_____

_____

_____

_____

_____

_____

The Swing

Robert Louis Stevenson

How do you like to go up in a swing,
   Up in the air so blue?
Oh, I do think it the pleasantest thing
   Ever a child can do!

Up in the air and over the wall,
   Till I can see so wide,
Rivers and trees and cattle and all
   Over the countryside—

Till I look down on the garden green,
   Down on the roof so brown—
Up in the air I go flying again,
   Up in the air and down!

The Swing

Objective

- Students will use information from the poem to determine where the story takes place.

Materials

- a cloze copy of the poem (page 65)
- a highlighter and a pencil for each student
- board or overhead space

Before Reading

1. Ask the students to describe some of the "pleasantest" things they have ever done.
2. List responses on the board.
3. Ask students to explain why they like these activities so much. What feelings do they have while they participate? Why is it so much fun?
4. Tell students you are going to give them some clues. They have to guess where you are. Say, "I hear an engine roaring. I see green and brown patches, tiny roads and cars. I feel a little excited. Where am I?" (*up in an airplane*) "I hear children screaming. I see a merry-go-round, bumper cars, and a hot dog stand. I feel excited. Where am I?" (*on top of the Ferris wheel*) "I hear sirens and car horns. I see lots of roofs, tiny roads and cars. I feel so small. Where am I?" (*on the top of a tall building*) What do all these places have in common? (*They are up high and someone is looking down.*)
5. Have students look at the title and ask them the following question: "What will the poem be about?" Look for reasons why the narrator likes this activity so much.

During Reading

1. First read the poem to the students, emphasizing phrasing, pausing, expression, and rhythm.
2. Read the three stanzas of the poem together orally several times.
3. Divide the class into three groups. Assign each group one stanza of the poem. Have the groups read the stanzas in order while the others follow along. Start with group one for the first reading, group two for the second reading, and group three for the third reading. To conclude, ask for volunteers to read the poem individually.

After Reading

- What does the author like to do? Why does he like to do this? Highlight details that explain why he likes it so much. Are any of these reasons the same as the reasons you gave above? Name some feelings he might have as he swings so high in the air.
- Ask the students to pretend they are the narrator of the poem. As a class, write a What Am I? riddle, as if the narrator made it up. Put it on the board. Discuss and save.
- Circle the details that describe what the narrator saw when he was high in the swing. Do you think he is in the city or the country? How do you know? Describe how things look different to the narrator if he sits in the swing with his feet on the ground.

Reading Support

This poem adapts well to choral reading. Have the students read it together. Encourage them to read with good expression in a sing-song way. Ask for volunteers to read separate stanzas on their own.

The Swing

Robert Louis Stevenson

How do you like to go up in a <u>swing</u>,

    Up in the air so blue?

Oh, I do think it the pleasantest _____

    Ever a child can do!

Up in the air and over the <u>wall</u>,

    Till I can see so wide,

Rivers and trees and cattle and _____

    Over the countryside—

Till I look down on the garden green,

    Down on the roof so <u>brown</u>—

Up in the air I go flying again,

    Up in the air and _____!

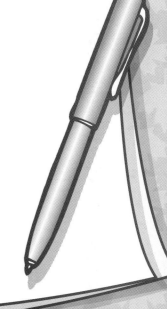

The Swing

Directions: Try to stump your classmates. Give them clues to some places you know or like to go. Can they guess where you are?

I see _____ .

I hear _____ .

I feel _____ .

Where am I?

I see _____ .

I hear _____ .

I feel _____ .

Where am I?

I see _____ .

I hear _____ .

I feel _____ .

Where am I?

Toys

Carolyn Sherwin Bailey

All up and down the land I go
With mother, making calls,
And sit in chairs so much too high
In strange and different halls,
And cannot think of things to say,
And feel so pleased to start away.

But when we come back home again,
I am so glad to see
The very oldest of the toys
All waiting there for me;
The horse who lost his tail, the blocks,
And all the soldiers in their box.

The horse cart with the broken shaft,
The doll who used to talk;
The little duck who ran so fast,
And now, can't even walk—
They all are friends, so kind and true,
Because of what they used to do.

And every day when I'm away,
I think they miss me so;
I really should not leave them once—
They're sensitive, I know.
And just to comfort them a mite,
I take them all to bed at night.

Toys

Objective

- Students will summarize the stanzas of the poem in their own words.

Materials

- a cloze copy of the poem (page 69)
- a highlighter and a pencil for each student
- board or overhead space

Before Reading

1. Open with a discussion of the students' favorite toys.
2. List student responses on the board or overhead.
3. Discuss reasons why they like their toys so much.
4. List student ideas for the following questions as well. What kinds of toys did children play with long ago? How have toys changed over the years? What are some good things about the changes? Some bad things?
5. Tell students that they should be ready to describe the toys the child plays with in the poem and how they compare to their own.

During Reading

1. After a whole-group choral practice, divide the class into two groups. The first group reads the first two lines of the poem with you, while the second group follows along. Then the second group reads the second two lines with you, while the first group follows along.
2. Continue alternating groups until the entire poem has been read. Repeat the same procedure, starting with group two the second time.

After Reading

- Highlight the toys named in the poem and the details that describe them. Verify and discuss. What toys are the same as your own? Which ones are different? Add new information to the chart above.
- For discussion: Who is telling the story? How does the narrator feel about his or her toys? How do you know? Do you think the narrator is a boy or a girl? What makes you think so? Are the toys old or new? How do you know?
- Ask how many have seen one of the *Toy Story* movies. What are the similarities between the movie and the poem? (*In both, the toys take on human qualities and seem to be real.*) Underline details in the poem proving the toys seem real to the child.

Reading Support

List the rhyming pairs from the poem on the board. Using student input, chart other words that rhyme with these pairs. What is a synonym for the words "a mite" in the last stanza? (*a little*)

Toys

Carolyn Sherwin Bailey

All up and down the land I go

With mother, making <u>calls</u>,

And sit in chairs so much too high

In strange and different _____,

And cannot think of things to say,

And feel so pleased to start away.

But when we come back home again,

I am so glad to <u>see</u>

The very oldest of the toys

All waiting there for _____;

The horse who lost his tail, the blocks,

And all the soldiers in their box.

The horse cart with the broken shaft,

The doll who used to <u>talk</u>;

The little duck who ran so fast,

And now, can't even _____—

They all are friends, so kind and <u>true</u>,

Because of what they used to _____.

And every day when I'm away,

I think they miss me <u>so</u>;

I really should not leave them once—

They're sensitive, I _____.

And just to comfort them a <u>mite</u>,

I take them all to bed at _____.

Toys

Directions: Reread the first stanza of the poem. Summarize the stanza in your own words. Write the summary in the space for stanza 1 below. Continue in the same manner for stanzas 2, 3, and 4.

Stanza 1: _____.

_____

_____

_____

Stanza 2: _____.

_____

_____

_____

Stanza 3: _____.

_____

_____

_____

Stanza 4: _____.

_____

_____

_____

Very Lovely

Rose Fyleman

Wouldn't it be lovely if the rain came down

Till the water was quite high over all the town?

If the cabs and buses all were set afloat,

And we had to go to school in a little boat?

Wouldn't it be lovely if it still should pour

And we all went up to live on the second floor?

If we saw the butcher sailing up the hill,

And we took the letters in at the window sill?

It's been raining, raining, all the afternoon;

All these things might happen really very soon.

If we woke to-morrow and found they had begun,

Wouldn't it be glorious? *Wouldn't* it be fun?

Very Lovely

Objective

- Students will demonstrate an understanding of the cause-effect relationship as it applies to the events in the story.

Materials

- a cloze copy of the poem (page 73)
- a highlighter and pencil for each student
- large chart paper
- overhead or board space

Before Reading

1. Introduce the topic "rainy days."
2. Discuss reasons why the students like rainy days, and reasons why they don't.
3. Tell students that cause/effect relationships occur when one event makes other events happen. On the board or overhead, list each of these events. Label the list "The Cause"—a rainy day, a flood, a frost, a snowstorm, a car accident, a hot sunny day, below zero temperatures, etc.
4. Create a second column labeled, "The Effects" With student input, record the effects of each one of these causes.
5. In "Very Lovely," the author describes a very rainy day. Tell students to be ready to discuss what the author wants to happen on this rainy afternoon.

During Reading

1. The teacher reads the first line of the poem, modeling good expression and phrasing, as the students follow along.
2. The students then echo back the first line, following along with their fingers.
3. Continue in the same manner until all lines have been read. Repeat as needed.
4. Conclude with a choral reading of the entire poem by the whole class.

After Reading

- Have students circle the event the author describes. Then have them highlight and discuss the effects that follow.
- For discussion: What event does the author describe? What are the effects of this event? What makes the author think all this will happen? How does she feel about the situation? Do you think she is being realistic? Why or why not? What is the setting of "Very Lovely"—where does it take place? When does it take place? Find details that make you think this is true.
- On scrap paper, have students write an alternate title for the poem. As the titles are read, students should be ready to defend their choices.

Reading Support

This poem adapts well to choral reading. Read the poem out loud together several times, clapping out the rhythm according to the phonemes as you read. Encourage reading in a sing-song way.

Very Lovely

Rose Fyleman

Wouldn't it be lovely if the rain came <u>down</u>

Till the water was quite high over all the _____?

If the cabs and buses all were set <u>afloat</u>,

And we had to go to school in a little _____?

Wouldn't it be lovely if it still should pour

And we all went up to live on the second floor?

If we saw the butcher sailing up the <u>hill</u>,

And we took the letters in at the window _____?

It's been raining, raining, all the afternoon;

All these things might happen really very soon.

If we woke to-morrow and found they had <u>begun</u>,

Wouldn't it be glorious? *Wouldn't* it be _____?

Very Lovely

Directions: Imagine that one day "The rain came down till the water was quite high over all your town." Write an entry in your journal describing what happened that day. Write your entry below. Be sure to include the following: when the rain started, how long it lasted, and some events that occurred in the morning, in the afternoon, in the evening, and that night.

Dear Journal,

_____

_____

_____

_____

_____

_____

_____

_____

Home

and

Family

Baby Sister

Helen Crooker Lawrence

I have a new little sister,

She's very, very small.

She listens to the things I say

But will not talk at all.

I surely wish she'd tell me things,

There's lots I want to know.

I wonder if she'd like to talk.

She surely likes to grow!

Until she does, I'll talk to her,

And though she is so wee—

I know she understands it all,

For she smiles back at me!

Baby Sister

Objective

- Students will demonstrate the ability to recognize methods of nonverbal communication.

Materials

- a cloze copy of the poem (page 78)
- a highlighter and a pencil for each student

Before Reading

1. Ask how many of the students have younger brothers or sisters at home. What do you remember about them when they were only a few months old? How did they communicate?

2. Babies have a language all of their own. They can communicate with us, even though they can't explain how they feel in words. This is called nonverbal communication. How did you know when your little brother or sister was happy? How did you know when he or she was sad?

3. Read to find out how the narrator of the poem communicates with her baby sister. What nonverbal communication does the baby use?

During Reading

1. Pair your students, putting a fluent reader with an early reader whenever possible.

2. The pairs take turns being reader and listener. The first reader reads the poem to the listener three times. At this time, the listener compliments the reader on what he feels the reader has done well (no negative comments are allowed).

3. The listener and the reader then switch roles, and follow the same procedure. Allow reading and rereading and switching of roles for an allotted time, 10–15 minutes for example.

After Reading

- Highlight the details in the poem that describe the baby. Discuss. Although the baby is very, very small, the narrator knows Baby Sister understands him or her. Highlight the details that show this to be true. How do you think the baby feels about her older sibling? Why do you think this is true?

- For discussion: What are some questions you think the narrator would want to ask the baby? What answers might the baby give if she could talk? Since the baby cannot talk yet, what is the narrator going to do in the meantime? Is this a good idea? Why or why not?

- Even if we do not talk about it, feelings are easy to recognize—in babies, older children, and adults. How could you tell if an older person is happy? Sad? Angry? Scared? Excited? Bored? Interested? Loving? What actions would they demonstrate in these situations? (particular facial expressions, hand or body movements)

- Ask student volunteers to act out some of the nonverbal communication methods discussed. See if their classmates can guess which ones they are interpreting.

Reading Support

Ask the students to circle the contractions in the poem. Ask "What two words are represented by each contraction?"

Baby Sister

Helen Crooker Lawrence

I have a new little sister,

She's very, very <u>small</u>.

She listens to the things I say

But will not talk at _____.

I surely wish she'd tell me things,

There's lots I want to <u>know</u>.

I wonder if she'd like to talk.

She surely likes to _____!

Until she does, I'll talk to her,

And though she is so <u>wee</u>—

I know she understands it all,

For she smiles back at _____!

Baby Sister

Directions: Choose one of the feelings listed below. Write a story about a time when you felt this way. In your story, be sure to describe what happened, and explain why you felt the way you did. How did others know what you were feeling?

Happy

Sad

Surprised

Excited

Angry

Scared

_____

_____

_____

_____

_____

_____

_____

_____

Do You Guess It Is I?

Eliza Lee Follen

I am a little thing;

I am not very high;

I laugh, dance and sing,

And sometimes I cry.

I have a little head

All covered o'er with hair,

And I hear what is said

With my two ears there.

On my two feet I walk;

I run too with ease;

With my little tongue I talk

Just as much as I please.

I have ten fingers too,

And just so many toes;

Two eyes to see through,

And but one little nose.

I've a mouth full of teeth,

Where my bread and milk go in;

And close by, underneath,

Is my little, round chin.

What is this little thing,

Not very, very high,

That can laugh, dance and sing?

Do you guess it is I?

A BABY

Do You Guess It Is I?

Objective

- Using details from the poem, students will guess whom it is about.

Materials

- a cloze copy of the poem (page 82)
- a highlighter and a pencil for each student
- word cards containing some -*ea* short and long vowel words. (Some short vowel examples: *head, heavy, ready, deaf, dread, thread, steady, breath, spread.* Some long vowel sound examples: *eat, each, meat, clean, neat, read, weak, deal, sea.*)

Before Reading

1. Play the game I Spy with the students, offering clues to objects around the room. (I Spy something that is . . . .)
2. Give one or two clues at a time until the object is guessed. Ask for student volunteers to do the same.
3. Tell the students that the poem they are about to read is like an I Spy riddle. They will be asked to figure the answer to the riddle. Have them listen carefully for clues that convey the answer. On their cloze activity page, tell them to write their guesses on the line at the end of the poem.

During Reading

1. Divide the class into six groups. Put readers of mixed reading ability in each group.
2. Assign each group one of the stanzas of the poem to practice several times.
3. When you feel fluency has been established, reconvene.
4. Group one reads stanza one, the rest of the class echoes by reading stanza one; group two reads stanza two, the rest of the class echoes stanza two, and so on until the whole poem has been read.
5. Close with a group choral reading of the entire poem.

After Reading

For discussion, ask the following question: "Who did you guess the poem was about?" Log responses on the board or overhead. Have the students highlight at least five clues that support their guesses. Discuss the clues they found. How many agreed with the author? Some may not agree at all. If so, talk about why they do not agree (for example, they might say the child in the poem sounds much older than a baby).

Reading Support

Have the students circle all the words in the poem that contain an –*ea*. On the board or overhead, categorize the words according to whether they have a short vowel or long vowel sound. Randomly pass out a mixture of long and short vowel -*ea* word cards. Ask students to add their word card to the column on the board that has the matching vowel sound. Read the columns of words together as a group.

Do You Guess It Is I?

Eliza Lee Follen

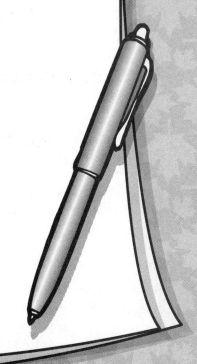

I am a little thing;
I am not very <u>high</u>;
I laugh, dance and sing,
And sometimes I _____.

I have a little head
All covered o'er with <u>hair</u>,
And I hear what is said
With my two ears _____.

On my two feet I walk;
I run too with <u>ease</u>;
With my little tongue I talk
Just as much as I _____.

I have ten fingers too,
And just so many <u>toes</u>;
Two eyes to see through,
And but one little _____.

I've a mouth full of teeth,
Where my bread and milk go <u>in</u>;
And close by, underneath,
Is my little, round _____.

What is this little thing,
Not very, very <u>high,</u>
That can laugh, dance and sing?
Do you guess it is _____?

I am a _____.

Do You Guess It Is I?

Directions: Write a riddle of your own similar to the one we just read. Fill in the blanks below with your clues. Then read your riddle to the class and see if they can guess your answer.

I Spy?

I spy something that is (little or big) _____.

It is not _____.

Sometimes it _____.

It has _____.

You can hear it_____.

You can watch it_____.

When you touch it, it feels _____.

It is a _____.

Grandma's Cookie Jar

Barbara Hanna

My grandma has a cookie jar
Up high upon a shelf
And when I go to visit her
She says, "Just help yourself."

So then I climb up on a chair
And reach up very tall,
And put my hand way down inside—
I'm careful not to fall.

Sometimes I find they're round and sweet;
Sometimes they're filled with spice;
And then again all sorts of shapes;
But any kind is nice.

When Grandma hears I'm coming soon,
She starts right in to bake,
And knows that I shall always like
Whatever kind she'll make.

Grandma's Cookie Jar

Objective

- Students will describe individual character traits that should be used toward deserving grandparents and older adults.

Materials

- a cloze copy of the poem (page 86)
- a highlighter and a pencil for each student
- board space or overhead
- microphone

Before Reading

1. Open a discussion on grandparents. Ask the students to share how they feel about their grandparents (or an older adult friend). Encourage them to talk about what they like best about their grandparents, activities they do with their grandparents, how they help their grandparents, how their grandparents help them, etc.

2. Impress on students the importance of positive character. Ask them to offer character traits they should especially display toward grandparents or older adults and why they are deserving.

3. Chart on the board or overhead. Log student responses.

4. Discuss for what each trait stands. Some examples are as follows:

    Honesty: Telling the truth and being trustworthy

    Caring: Showing affection and concern

    Cooperation: Getting along and doing what is expected

    Respect: Treating others as you want to be treated

    Fairness: Treating everyone the same

5. Have students predict what "Grandmother's Cookie Jar" will be about. Ask them to be ready to explain how the characters in the poem feel about each other and which character traits they display.

During Reading

1. Modeling good fluency, read the poem to the students two or three times.

2. Divide the class into four groups. Have each group practice reading the poem several times. When you feel they have enough confidence, bring the class together in a circle.

3. Hand a microphone to the student you choose to start. This student reads the first line of the poem into the microphone, passes the microphone on to the next student to read the second line, and so on around the circle, until the whole poem has been read. (Those who are not reading should be following along.)

4. Repeat as often as time allows, starting with a new student for each reading.

After Reading

For discussion: Were your predictions correct? How does the child in the poem feel about his or her grandmother? How do you know? How does the grandmother feel about her grandchild? How do you know? Which character traits does the grandmother display toward her grandchild? The child toward his or her grandmother? Highlight details in the poem that show this is true. In what ways do you show positive character toward your own grandparents and older adult friends?

Reading Support

Make flashcards of all sight words in the poem. Have students practice reading the flashcards.

Grandma's Cookie Jar
Barbara Hanna

My grandma has a cookie jar

Up high upon a <u>shelf</u>

And when I go to visit her

She says, "Just help your _____."

So then I climb up on a chair

And reach up very <u>tall</u>,

And put my hand way down inside—

I'm careful not to _____.

Sometimes I find they're round and sweet;

Sometimes they're filled with <u>spice</u>;

And then again all sorts of shapes;

But any kind is _____.

When Grandma hears I'm coming soon,

She starts right in to <u>bake</u>,

And knows that I shall always like

Whatever kind she'll _____.

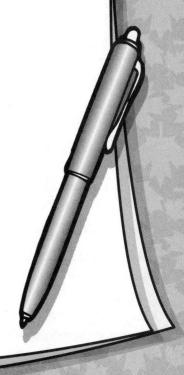

Grandma's Cookie Jar

Directions: Pretend that your parents or guardians are away for the weekend, and you are staying with your grandparents or an older adult friend. During your stay, write what can you do to show that you are . . .

Cooperative _____
_____
_____

Honest _____
_____
_____

Respectful _____
_____
_____

Caring _____
_____
_____

Fair _____
_____
_____

I Dreamed I Was a Snowman

Eleanor Dennis

Of all the dreams I ever had,
The funniest of them yet
Is one I dreamed about last night,
I never will forget.

I dreamed I was a snowman
Who started for a walk,
And every time I saw someone
I'd stop for a while to talk.

I met a pretty little girl
Who wanted me to play.
She looked so lonesome all alone
And so I said I'd stay.

I went into the house with her,
And sat down in a chair,
But when I started up to go,
I wasn't anywhere.

I couldn't find myself at all,
My brain was in a muddle.
For not a bit of me was left
But just a great big puddle.

I Dreamed I Was a Snowman

Objective

- Students will determine whether the poem is fantasy or reality.

Materials

- a cloze copy of the poem (page 90)
- a pencil and paper for each student
- board space or overhead

Before Reading

1. Write the headings Fantasy and Reality on the board or overhead.
2. Talk with the students about dreams. Discuss events or happenings that can influence dreams. Have them tell about some funny dreams they have had, as well as some sad ones and some scary ones. Which dreams could actually have happened? Which ones could not? Why or why not? Log a few examples for each under the headings above.
3. Lead to a discussion as to the difference between fantasy and reality. (*Fantasy is impossible in real life. Reality could really happen.*)
4. Have students look at the title of the poem. Have them predict what it will be about. Will it be fantasy or reality? How do they know? What do they think might happen in this dream?

During Reading

1. Divide the class into pairs, combining a fluent reader (Reader 1) with an early reader (Reader 2).
2. Reader 1 reads the poem to Reader 2 three times. Reader 2 follows along, pointing to the words. Reader 2 then reads the poem to Reader 1 three times. Reader 1 points and follows along this time.
3. Conclude with a choral reading of the poem by pairs: the pairs take turns reading two lines of the poem until the whole poem has been read.
4. Repeat, starting with a different pair each time the poem is read.

After Reading

- Ask students, "Were your predictions correct? What type of dream does the narrator have? How do you know? Is it real or fantasy? Highlight the details in the poem that lead you to this conclusion."
- For discussion, use the following questions: Explain what actually happens in the last stanza of the poem. How does the snowman get to this point? What events along the way cause him to melt? What could the snowman have done to stay "alive?" What makes the dream so funny?
- Ask students, "Can you think of a story the narrator might have read before going to bed that influenced his dream? (*Frosty the Snowman*) What details make you think so?"

Reading Support

Have students circle the compound words in the poem. What two words are combined in each case? Jot down on the board or overhead other compound words that are familiar to them.

I Dreamed I Was a Snowman

Eleanor Dennis

Of all the dreams I ever had,
The funniest of them <u>yet</u>
Is one I dreamed about last night,
I never will for _____.

I dreamed I was a snowman
Who started for a <u>walk</u>,
And every time I saw someone
I'd stop for a while to _____.

I met a pretty little girl
Who wanted me to <u>play</u>.
She looked so lonesome all alone
And so I said I'd _____.

I went into the house with her,
And sat down in a <u>chair</u>,
But when I started up to go,
I wasn't any _____.

I couldn't find myself at all,
My brain was in a <u>muddle</u>.
For not a bit of me was left
But just a great big _____.

I Dreamed I Was a Snowman

Directions: Think about a dream you have had. List as many details as you remember that happened in your dream. Share your dream with the class.

1. _____

2. _____

3. _____

4. _____

5. _____

6. _____

7. _____

8. _____

9. _____

10. _____

The Good Night Sheep

Carolyn Sherwin Bailey

If you shut your two eyes

and lie ever so quiet,

Counting them soft and slow,

One little, two little,

three little sheep,

As down through the field they go;

Four little, five little,

six little seven

Trotting so gray and small—

One and then two,

and then six and then seven,

Jumping across the wall;

Some of them faster,

but mostly slower,

Eight little, nine little, ten.

Ten little sheep—

and you have to stop counting—

I think that you go to sleep then.

The Good Night Sheep

Objectives

- Students will summarize the details of the poem in correct sequential order.
- Students will predict what will happen next.

Materials

- a cloze copy of the poem (page 94)
- highlighter and pencil for each student
- board or overhead space

Before Reading

1. For discussion, ask students the following questions: What time do you go to bed on school nights? On weekends? Why are the times different? Do any of you ever have trouble falling asleep? Why does this happen? What are some things you can do to make falling asleep easier?

2. Students should be ready to describe the method for falling asleep the narrator recommends.

During Reading

1. As the students follow along, read the entire poem to the students, modeling good expression, correct phrasing, and voice inflection.

2. Read the poem to them a second time, this time holding up the number of fingers required as the number of sheep change.

3. Now have the students read the poem with you. (They hold up their fingers also, as the number of sheep change.)

4. Finally, allow the class to read the poem together without your assistance.

5. Then, ask for volunteers to read a stanza, or the whole poem, using the hand motions you have practiced.

After Reading

- Ask students the following questions: "What method of falling asleep does the author recommend? How does this method work? Who do you think is narrating the poem? What makes you think so? To whom is the narrator speaking? What gives you this idea?"

- Have the students copy, as you write on the board or overhead, "Five Steps to Falling Asleep," numbering 1–5 underneath. Divide the class into pairs. Have each pair work together to summarize the steps the narrator describes. Reconvene. Discuss and come to an agreement as to what the five steps should be. (You close your eyes, you lie quiet, you count the sheep, you stop counting, you go to sleep.)

Reading Support

Have students do a number word search. Have students highlight the number words in the poem. Verify and log how many times each number word appears. Which number word occurs the most? Which number word occurs the least?

The Good Night Sheep
Carolyn Sherwin Bailey

If you shut your two eyes

And lie ever so quiet,

Counting them soft and <u>slow</u>,

One little, two little,

Three little sheep,

As down through the field they _____;

Four little, five little,

Six little seven

Trotting so gray and <u>small</u>—

One and then two,

And then six and then seven,

Jumping across the _____;

Some of them faster,

But mostly slower,

Eight little, nine little, <u>ten</u>.

Ten little sheep—

And you have to stop counting—

I think that you go to sleep _____.

The Good Night Sheep

Directions: In the story boxes below, illustrate the events of stanzas 1–3. Then, write a caption inside the box to go with each picture. What do you think happened in the end? Draw your idea in Story Box 4.

Story Box 1	**Story Box 2**
Story Box 3	**Story Box 4**

The Naughty Boy

Carolyn Sherwin Bailey

I threw my bread and butter,
I slammed the nursery door,
And all my pleasant playthings
Are lying on the floor.

But now it's growing dusky,
I am sitting all alone;
Not any one will speak to me
Because of what I've done.

The sun behind the orchard
Has hurried off to see
If all the other little boys
Are naughty boys like me.

Oh, mother, come and kiss me,
Don't look so very sad;
I'll pick up every single toy,
I'm sorry I was bad.

The Naughty Boy

Objectives

- Students will demonstrate knowledge of the aspects of responsibility.
- Students will recognize the importance of being responsible both at home and at school.

Materials

- a cloze copy of the poem (page 98)
- a highlighter and pencil for each student
- chart paper
- overhead or board space

Before Reading

1. Discuss the meaning of responsibility. (*being accountable for one's actions, being dependable and reliable in carrying out tasks*)
2. Web on the board or overhead several aspects of responsibility: what it means, why it is important, responsibilities the students have at home, responsibilities they have at school, etc.
3. Discuss responsible actions they have seen their classmates, brothers, or sisters take. Have they noticed any irresponsible behaviors in the classrooms or at home? What actions should have been taken in each case?
4. Tell the students to be thinking about the narrator as they read the poem. Does he demonstrate responsible behavior?

During Reading

1. Read the entire poem to the students first. To make the practice a little more fun, alternate the loudness of your voice, reading the first line louder than the second. Continue this pattern throughout.
2. Discuss the pattern with the class.
3. Join the students in a group choral reading conducted in the same manner, alternating loud and soft lines.
4. Reread several times.
5. Ask for volunteers to read the poem individually.

After Reading

- For discussion, ask students the following questions: Where is the narrator? What is the time of day? Who is with him? How is the family treating him? Does the narrator demonstrate responsible behavior? How do you know? Have students highlight behaviors in the poem that show he does not.
- For discussion, ask students the following questions: Is the narrator punished for his behavior? If so, how? Have students highlight details in the poem to support their answers. Do you feel the punishment is appropriate? Do you think the narrator learns his lesson? How do you know? What will he do next time?

Reading Support

Have students circle specific sight words as you call them off.

The Naughty Boy
Carolyn Sherwin Bailey

I threw my bread and butter,

I slammed the nursery <u>door</u>,

And all my pleasant playthings

Are lying on the _____.

But now it's growing dusky,

I am sitting all alone;

Not any one will speak to me

Because of what I've done.

The sun behind the orchard

Has hurried off to <u>see</u>

If all the little boys

Are naughty boys like _____.

Oh, mother, come and kiss me,

Don't look so very <u>sad</u>;

I'll pick up every single toy,

I'm sorry I was _____.

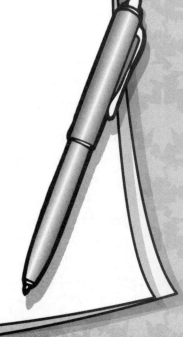

The Naughty Boy

Directions: At the end, the boy in the poem apologizes by saying he is sorry for what he has done.

> (Last Stanza)
>
> Oh, mother, come and kiss me,
>
> Don't look so very sad;
>
> I'll pick up every single toy,
>
> I'm sorry I was bad.

What do you think is going to happen now? Will he pick up his toys? Will his mother forgive him? Will he be allowed to come out of his room? Add one or two more stanzas to the poem, indicating what you think is going to happen next. Try to keep the rhyming pattern by using rhyming words at the end of the second and fourth lines.

Mother's Little Girl

Carolyn Sherwin Bailey

Mother knows a little girl,
Mother won't tell who—
Helps with all the many things
A mother has to do.

Sings to baby when he cries,
Builds his shaky blocks,
Irons grandma's handkerchiefs,
Folds up father's socks.

Picks the berries, dusts the hall
Neat as neat can be,
Draws out grandpa's easy chair,
Sets the plates for tea.

Buttons little sister's dress,
Lets her come and play
When another little girl
Sometimes runs away.

Mother knows a little girl.
Don't you wish you knew
Which it is who helps her so?
Mother won't tell who.

Mother's Little Girl

Objectives

- Students will identify the details in the poem that demonstrate responsibility.
- Students will compare the actions of the characters in "The Naughty Boy" (page 96) and "Mother's Little Girl."

Materials

- a cloze copy of the poem (page 102)
- a highlighter and pencil for each student

Before Reading

1. Review responsibility: what it means, why it is important. Review responsible behaviors exhibited at home and at school.
2. Have students list on scrap paper things they do at home to help. Share. Save for future reference.
3. Tell the students to be ready to explain how the little girl in the poem and "The Naughty Little Boy" (page 96) are the same and how they are different.

During Reading

1. Modeling good fluency, read the poem to the class while the students follow along.
2. Next, have the whole class read the poem chorally.
3. Finally, gather the class in a circle, choosing one student to begin. Starting with the student you have chosen, take turns having the students read the lines of the poem in order, as their classmates follow along.
4. Choose a second student to begin a second reading.
5. Repeat as proficiency demands or time allows.

After Reading

- Is the narrator of this poem responsible? How do you know? Highlight details in the poem to show that she is. How does she compare to the naughty boy? How are they different? How are they the same? How does she compare to you?
- Have students go back to the list of the things the students did at home to help. Ask them, "What are some extra things you could do? Add these to your list. Pick one or two to go home and do today."

Reading Support

Have students circle the words in the poem that begin with the following blends: *br–, cr–, dr–, gr–*. Chart the words on chart paper in separate columns. With student input, add other words to each column that begin with the same blend. Hang on the wall or save for future review.

Mother's Little Girl
Carolyn Sherwin Bailey

Mother knows a little girl,

Mother won't tell <u>who</u>—

Helps with all the many things

A mother has to _____.

Sings to baby when he cries,

Builds his shaky <u>blocks</u>,

Irons grandma's handkerchiefs,

Folds up father's _____.

Picks the berries, dusts the hall

Neat as neat can <u>be</u>,

Draws out grandpa's easy chair,

Sets the plates for _____.

Buttons little sister's dress,

Lets her come and <u>play</u>

When another little girl

Sometimes runs _____.

Mother knows a little girl.

Don't you wish you <u>knew</u>

Which it is who helps her so?

Mother won't tell _____.

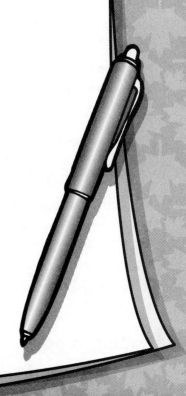

Mother's Little Girl

Directions: Using the Venn diagram below, list details that show how the main character in "Mother's Little Girl" and the main character in "The Naughty Boy" are the same and how they are different. Use the overlapped inner circles to list things that are the same. Use the outer circles to list things that are different.

The Naughty Boy

Mother's Little Girl

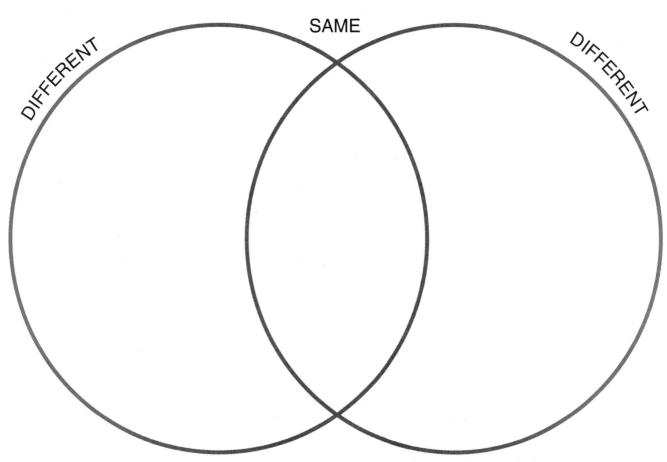

No One Heard Him Call

Dorothy Aldis

He went down to the woodshed
To put his bike away.
There was no moon. There were no stars.
He ran the whole dark way.

And when he hurried back again
The porch light had gone out!
He couldn't find the doorknob,
So then he gave a shout.

It wasn't very loud, though,
And no one heard him call.
He pounded with his knuckles;
Still no one came at all.

But then where he was standing
A *light* came streaming wide:
"My goodness is that you?" she said.

And he was safe inside!

No One Heard Him Call

Objectives

- Students will describe the main character's feelings
- Students will explain how and why the main character's feelings changed.

Materials

- a cloze copy of the poem (page 106)
- a colored highlighter and a pencil for each student

Before Reading

1. Darkness is a scary thing for some children. Discuss reasons why this is true.

   Ask the students to tell about times when they have been scared of the dark. Why were they scared in these situations? How did they overcome their fear? Did someone help them do this?

2. As the poem is read, tell students to be ready with details to show how the child in the poem feels in the beginning and how his feelings have changed by the end.

During Reading

1. Read the poem to the students. As you read, give extra emphasis to the pronouns *I, my, me, I've, I'll,* and *I'm.* Did the students hear the pattern? Read again, if they did not.

2. On their copies of the poem, ask the students to highlight, underline, or circle all the pronoun referents mentioned above. Validate.

3. Conduct a group choral reading, asking the students to echo the emphasis you modeled above.

4. Practice several times.

5. Divide the class into four groups. Assign each group a stanza to read to the rest of the class, while those who are not reading follow along.

After Reading

Reread each stanza of the poem orally, one by one. Ask how the main character feels at each of these points in the story. Highlight details that make the child feel this way. How did the child's feelings change by the end of the story? Highlight details that contributed to this change.

Play the teacher game. In this game, the students take over the role of the teacher. To introduce the game, write the following six question words on the board: Who? What? Where? Why? When? How? Give the students the opportunity to ask questions of their classmates. The questions they ask must begin with one of the words in the list, and the answer must be found in the poem. The classmate who answers each question may be designated to ask the next one.

Reading Support

Divide the class into groups. Assign one of the rhyming patterns in the poem to each group. Have each group list other words of the same pattern. Check for accuracy. Have students transfer the words in their list to word cards. Use later in a center for vowel activities.

No One Heard Him Call

Dorothy Aldis

He went down to the woodshed

To put his bike <u>away</u>

There was no moon. There were no stars.

He ran the whole dark _____.

And when he hurried back again

The porch light had gone <u>out</u>!

He couldn't find the doorknob,

So then he gave a _____.

It wasn't very loud, though,

And no one heard him <u>call</u>.

He pounded with his knuckles;

Still no one came at _____.

But then where he was standing

A *light* came streaming <u>wide</u>:

"My goodness is that you?" she said.

And he was safe _____!

No One Heard Him Call

Directions: Fill in the chart below, describing in a few words what happens and how the child feels at each point in the story. Use details from the poem to help you. Then finish the statement below.

Stanza	What Happens?	How Does the Child Feel?
1		
2		
3		
4		

The child's feelings in the poem change because . . .

_____

_____

_____

_____

_____

A Real Santa Claus

Frank Dempster Sherman

Santa Claus, I hang for you
By the mantel, stockings two;
One for me and one to go
To another boy I know.

There's a chimney in the town
You have never traveled down.
Should you chance to enter there
You would find a room all bare;

Not a stocking could you spy
Matters not how you might try;
And the shoes you'd find are such
As no boy would care for much.

In a broken bed you'd see
Someone just about like me,
Dreaming of the pretty toys
Which you bring to other boys,
And to him a Christmas seems
Merry only in his dreams.

All he dreams then, Santa Claus,
Stuff the stocking with because
When it's filled up to the brim
I'll be Santa Claus to him!

A Real Santa Claus

Objective

- After reading the poem, students will recognize the lesson it teaches.

Materials

- a cloze copy of the poem (page 109)
- 10 large stocking shapes, cut from construction or heavy paper, each with a rhyming pattern from the poem written on it
- a highlighter and a pencil for each student
- chart paper, overhead, or board space

Before Reading

1. Have the students brainstorm thoughts that come to mind when they see the word *Christmas*. As responses are given, jot them on chart paper, the board, or overhead.
2. Without telling the students, group them according to topic. (Some examples of topics that might come up are Decorations, Gift Giving, Santa Claus, Christmas Eve, Parties, etc.) Ask volunteers to think of topics for each group of responses. Verify and discuss.
3. If the students did not come up with the "True Meaning of Christmas," or something similar, as one of the topics, add that to the chart. Then ask for ideas that come to mind. Elicit ideas such as the following: giving is better than receiving, etc.
4. Ask students to predict from the title what they think the poem is going to be about.

During Reading

1. This is a perfect poem to perform for an audience at holiday time. In order to prepare, read the poem to the students, modeling good fluency. Emphasize in your reading the feelings of the main character.
2. Conduct a group choral reading of the poem, allowing your students to echo your expression and then read chorally a second time.
3. Divide the class into five groups of mixed ability. Assign alternating stanzas of the poem to each group. Have the groups practice their stanzas until fluency is achieved.
4. Reconvene in a circle for a rereading of the poem. As each group reads its assigned stanza, the members stand up. Props and hand motions may be added, if desired.

After Reading

For discussion, ask the following questions: What is the poem about? Were your predictions correct? Why does the narrator hang two stockings by his mantel? Highlight details in the poem that describe the poor boy's room. What do these details tell you about him? How do you think he feels on Christmas Eve and why? What are the poor boy's dreams for Christmas? What should Santa put in his stocking? What other Christmas presents do you think he needs? What could you do to help him? What does the narrator mean when he says, "I'll be Santa Claus to him"? How do you think the narrator will feel when he delivers the stocking? How do you think the poor boy will feel when his friend arrives? What is the lesson we can learn from this story? (*Helping others is important because it shows that we care.*) What positive character traits does the narrator possess?

Reading Support

Divide the group into ten groups. Give each group a stocking shape with one of the rhyming pairs written on it. Have the groups add additional rhyming words to their stockings. Hang the stockings around the room or use for a bulletin board display.

A Real Santa Claus

Frank Dempster Sherman

Santa Claus, I hang for you

By the mantel, stockings two;

One for me and one to <u>go</u>

To another boy I _____.

There's a chimney in the <u>town</u>

You have never traveled _____.

Should you chance to enter <u>there</u>

You would find a room all _____;

Not a stocking could you <u>spy</u>

Matters not how you might _____;

And the shoes you'd find are <u>such</u>

As no boy would care for_____.

In a broken bed you'd <u>see</u>

Someone just about like _____,

Dreaming of the pretty <u>toys</u>

Which you bring to other _____,

And to him a Christmas <u>seems</u>

Merry only in his _____.

All he dreams then, Santa Claus,

Stuff the stocking with because

When it's filled up to the <u>brim</u>

I'll be Santa Claus to _____!

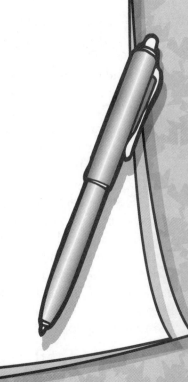

A Real Santa Claus

Directions: Illustrate the poor boy's room as it looked before Christmas. Use details from the poem in your picture.

Directions: Illustrate the poor boy's room after Christmas. Include in your picture items you think Santa put in his stocking and other gifts he needs and deserves.

The Sad Shoes
Dorothy Aldis

My poor old shoes are on the floor.
Last winter they were new.
Now I don't wear them any more.
Too many holes came through.

Today they had a nice time though
Climbing up a tree:
Tomorrow they'll be thrown away
And cannot play with me.

And doesn't this seem sad to you?
And do they maybe know?
I think perhaps they do—they lean
Upon each other so.

The Sad Shoes

Objectives

- Students will recognize the main idea of the poem.
- Students will locate details to support the main idea.

Materials

- a copy of the cloze version of the poem (page 114)
- a highlighter and a pencil for each student
- large chart paper, whiteboard, or blackboard space

Before Reading

1. Before handing out the poem, write the title of the poem on the board.
2. Ask the students to guess what the poem is going to be about. List their ideas on the board and save for later reference.
3. Ask students to talk about a favorite pair of shoes. At what age did they have this pair of shoes? What did the shoes look like? Why did they like these shoes so much?
4. Have the students be ready to tell the main idea of the poem.

During Reading

1. Assign a reading buddy to each of your students from another classroom, at least two grade levels ahead. (It would be beneficial if the older student could be given a copy of the poem ahead of time to practice.)
2. Have the older student read the poem to the younger student one or two times, modeling good expression, phrasing, and intonation, while the younger student points to the words and follows along. Next, echoing the expression he has just heard, the younger student reads the poem to the older student several times.
3. Finally, volunteers read the poem to their classmates, who continue following along.

After Reading

- Go back to the list of student guesses above. Which guesses were correct? Which guesses were not? Why did the narrator have to throw away her shoes?
- Highlight the details in the poem that describe the shoes. Why do you think it bothers the narrator so much to throw them away? How long did she have them? How did they get so worn out? How does she feel about them?
- Discuss the main idea of the poem. (*Giving up an old pair of shoes is like losing an old friend.*) Highlight the details in the poem that support the main idea. Discuss and verify the responses.
- Discuss ways old shoes and old friends are alike. Log responses and save.

Reading Support

Find and highlight the three contractions in the poem. Ask for the two words for which each contraction stands. Have students volunteer additional contractions that they know.

The Sad Shoes
Dorothy Aldis

My poor old shoes are on the floor.

Last winter they were <u>new</u>.

Now I don't wear them any more.

Too many holes came _____.

Today they had a nice time though

Climbing up a <u>tree</u>:

Tomorrow they'll be thrown away

And cannot play with _____.

And doesn't this seem sad to you?

And do they maybe <u>know</u>?

I think perhaps they do—they lean

Upon each other _____.

The Sad Shoes

Directions: Using the description in the poem to help you, draw and color an illustration of the author's "Sad Shoes." Write a few sentences to go with your picture. In your sentences, explain why the shoes are sad and why the author is sorry to see them go.

_____

_____

_____

_____

_____

_____

With a Friend

Vivian Gouled

I can talk with a friend
And walk with a friend
And share my umbrella in the rain.

I can play with a friend
And stay with a friend
And learn with a friend
And explain.

I can eat with a friend
And compete with a friend
And even sometimes disagree.

I can ride with a friend
And take pride with a friend
A friend can mean so much to me!

With a Friend

Objectives

- Students will distinguish the attributes of the character trait, "Caring."
- Student will demonstrate ways they can apply this trait towards others.

Materials

- a cloze copy of the poem (page 118)
- large chart paper, overhead, or board space
- a highlighter and a pencil for each student
- a copy of the book *Friends* by Helme Heine (Margaret K. McElderry Books, an Imprint of Simon and Schuster Children's Publishing Division, New York, 1982) or any other book on friends

Before Reading

1. Write the following incomplete phrases on the board, chart paper, or overhead, leaving space for student responses in between:

    Good friends are important because . . . .

    A good friend is always . . . .

    I can be a good friend by . . . .

2. As you record student responses, discuss each phrase as it relates to the positive character trait of caring. Encourage adjectives such as kind, thoughtful, trustworthy, and forgiving, etc. for the second phrase. Encourage concepts such as sharing, listening, helping, etc., for the third phrase. Save.

3. Read *Friends* by Helme Heine, or any other book on friends, to the students. Add attributes mentioned in the book to the chart. (*Friends stick together, decide things together, share things together, and are always fair.*)

4. Tell the students to be ready to discuss ways the author of "With a Friend" suggests we can show our friends we care.

During Reading

1. Read the poem to the students. (To add an element of fun, read alternate lines fast and slow.)

2. Have the students practice reading the poem a few times with you, following the fast and slow pattern.

3. Ask for volunteers to read the poem to the class individually or in groups.

After Reading

For discussion: What is different about the rhymes in this poem? (*They are in the middle of the stanza.*) What is the most important detail the author wants us to remember about friends? (*It is important to have good friends.*) Highlight ways we can show our friends we care. Are any of these already recorded in the chart? Are there any new ones to add?

Reading Support

Have students circle instances of the following sight words as you call them out: *I, a, and, can, in, the,* and *with*. Which sight word does the author use the most? Which one does she use the least?

With a Friend
Vivian Gouled

I can <u>talk</u> with a friend

And _____ with a friend

And share my umbrella in the rain.

I can <u>play</u> with a friend

And _____ with a friend

And learn with a friend

And explain.

I can <u>eat</u> with a friend

And _____ with a friend

And even sometimes disagree.

I can <u>ride</u> with a friend

And take _____with a friend

A friend can mean so much to me!

With a Friend

Directions: Using the friendly letter format, write a letter to one of your friends. In your letter, explain why he or she means so much to you. Use ideas from the chart, the book, and the poem to help you. Include things you do for each other that show you care.

Our

World

Today

I'd Like to Be A Lighthouse

Rachel Field

I'd like to be a lighthouse

    All scrubbed and painted white.

I'd like to be a lighthouse

    And stay awake all night.

To keep my eye on everything

    That sails my patch of sea;

I'd like to be a lighthouse

    With the ships all watching me.

I'd Like to Be A Lighthouse

Objective
- Students will locate descriptive details in the text.

Materials
- a cloze copy of the poem (page 123)
- *Beacons of Light* by Gail Gibbons, (William Morrow and Co., 1990) or another book on lighthouses
- highlighter and pencil for each student
- transparency copy of the poem
- large chart paper or overhead

Before Reading
1. Ask the students if they could change places with another person, animal, or thing, who or what would it be? List their ideas on the board.
2. Discuss the reasons for their choices. Ask how their lives would change if they were able to do this.
3. Ask students what they know about lighthouses. Use a "What I Know/What I Learned" Knowledge Chart to log responses. (See "The Sun's Journey" on page 138 for an example.) Read *Beacons of Light*, or another book on lighthouses, to the class. Students can now provide additional information for the chart.
4. Discuss the title of the poem with the students. Ask what they think the poem is going to be about.

During Reading
1. Read the poem out loud to the students as they follow along. Pause briefly between the phrases in each line.
2. Pair the students. Ask them to work together, putting slash marks between the phrases on their copies of the poem.
3. Using a transparency on the overhead, discuss and validate. Reconvene. Read the poem chorally with the group several times. Ask for volunteers of individuals or groups to read the poem on their own.

After Reading
- Ask students the following questions: What is the poem about? Was your guess correct?
- Ask students to highlight the details in the poem that describe lighthouses. Verify and discuss. Check the Knowledge Chart to see if any of these details are there. Add to the chart if they are not. Have the students highlight the details in the poem that show why the narrator wanted to be a lighthouse. Discuss these as well.
- For discussion, ask the following questions: Imagine a lighthouse having feelings. How would a lighthouse feel on a cold winter night? During a powerful storm? In the middle of night? When the sun is setting? On a warm summer day? Poll the class to see how many might like to change places with a lighthouse as the narrator wants to do. Discuss reasons why they would or would not like to do this.

Reading Support
Circle long vowel words in the poem. Categorize these words by vowel sound on chart paper or on the board. Have students volunteer other long vowel words for each category and add to the lists.

I'd Like to Be A Lighthouse
Rachel Field

I'd like to be a lighthouse

All scrubbed and painted <u>white</u>.

I'd like to be a lighthouse

And stay awake all _____.

To keep my eye on everything

That sails my patch of <u>sea</u>;

I'd like to be a lighthouse

With the ships all watching _____.

I'd Like to Be A Lighthouse

Directions: Pretend you are a ship's captain far out at sea on a stormy night. In a few sentences, describe how you are feeling and how the lighthouse will help you. Create an illustration to go with your story.

The Moon

Eliza Lee Follen

Oh, look at the moon!

She is shining up there;

Oh, mother, she looks

Like a lamp in the air.

Last week she was smaller

And shaped like a bow;

But now she's grown bigger

And round as an O.

Pretty Moon, pretty Moon,

How you shine on the door

And make it all bright

On my bedroom floor.

You shine on my playthings,

And show me their place,

And I love to look up

At your pretty bright face.

And there is a star

Close by you, and maybe

That small twinkling star

Is your little baby.

The Moon

Objectives

- Students will locate facts which support the narrator's feelings toward the moon.
- Students will identify the similes the author uses.

Materials

- a cloze copy of the poem (page 127)
- *The Moon Book* by Gail Gibbons (Holiday House, NY, 1997), or any nonfiction book(s) on the moon
- a highlighter and pencil for each student
- chart paper, overhead, or board space

Before Reading

1. On the board, chart paper, or overhead, create a web or knowledge chart titled, "The Moon." (See "The Sun's Journey" on page 138 for an example of a knowledge chart.)

2. Discuss and log information the students already know. Details might include what the moon looks like, its different shapes (phases), when it is seen, how we see it, moon exploration, etc.

3. Tell students to be ready with details from the poem that prove exactly how the narrator feels toward the moon.

During Reading

1. Read the poem to students using fluency techniques. Add the element of excitement to your reading and discussion. Read chorally with the students a few times.

3. Conduct a 60 second-timed reading: As the students point to the words and whisper read to themselves, time them for 60 seconds. When the time is up, say stop. Have them mark the last word they read. Do another 60 second-timed reading. Have them mark where they finished this time as well. Repeat the 60 second-timed reading several times. After each timed reading, the readers should finish farther ahead.

After Reading

- For discussion, ask the following questions: "What two moon shapes does the author mention? Highlight them both. What does the author mean when she says the moon is 'shaped like a bow'? (*It is shaped like the bow in bow and arrow.*) Do you know what the phases the 'O' and the 'bow' represent? Are there any other phases that you know of? (*Add the responses to the knowledge chart above. Responses will be verified in the next activity.*) How does the author feel about the moon? How do you know? Highlight the details that prove she feels this way."

- Discuss the comparisons the author makes (comparing the moon to a lamp in the air and a bow). Are these good comparisons? Why or why not? When an author uses a comparison like this, it is called a *simile*. What other similes could the author use?

Reading Support

Students circle words in the poem that begin with the *sh–* sound. They volunteer other words they know that begin with the *sh–* sound for you to list on the board.

The Moon

Eliza Lee Follen

Oh, look at the moon!

She is shining up <u>there</u>;

Oh, mother, she looks

Like a lamp in the _____.

Last week she was smaller

And shaped like a <u>bow</u>;

But now she's grown bigger

And round as an _____.

Pretty Moon, pretty Moon,

How you shine on the <u>door</u>

And make it all bright

On my bedroom _____.

You shine on my playthings,

And show me their <u>place</u>,

And I love to look up

At your pretty bright _____.

And there is a star

Close by you, and <u>maybe</u>

That small twinkling star

Is your little _____.

 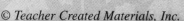

The Moon

Directions: Illustrate each stanza of the poem in the spaces provided. Include details from the stanza in each picture.

Oh, look at the moon!

She is shining up there;

Oh, mother, she looks

Like a lamp in the air.

Last week she was smaller

And shaped like a bow;

But now she's grown bigger

And round as an O.

Pretty Moon, pretty Moon,

How you shine on the door

And make it all bright

On my bedroom floor.

You shine on my playthings,

And show me their place,

And I love to look up

At your pretty bright face.

And there is a star

Close by you, and maybe

That small twinkling star

Is your little baby.

Our Flag

Aileen Fisher

How bright our flag
against the sky
atop its flagpole
straight and high.

How bright the red, the white, the blue,
with what they stand for
shining through,

More meaningful
as years go by . . .
how bright, how bright,
the flag we fly.

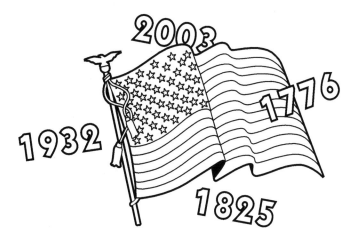

"Our Flag" from SKIP AROUND THE YEAR by Aileen Fisher.
Copyright 1967 by Thomas Y Crowell. Used by permission of
Marian Reiner for the Boulder Public Library Foundation.

Our Flag

Objective

- Students will determine the main idea the author is suggesting.

Materials

- a cloze copy of the poem (page 131)
- a pencil and a highlighter for each student
- a copy of *The American Flag* by Patricia Ryon Quiri (Children's Press, 1998) or any nonfiction book on the American flag
- large chart paper or overhead

Before Reading

1. Let students know that the poem they are going to read next is about the American flag.

2. Open a guided discussion by having several questions prewritten on large chart paper or on the overhead, such as the following: What does the United States flag look like? Why do we fly it? What are some rules to follow? What does it represent? What do the stars represent? What do the stripes represent? What does the red represent? What does the white represent? What does the blue represent? Log student responses.

3. Read *The American Flag* (or parts of it), or any other book on flags, as time permits, to the students. Verify, change, or correct responses given in the discussion above. (*Our flag is a symbol of freedom and stands for the land the people and the government. The stars stand for the fifty states, the thirteen stripes stand for the 13 original colonies, the red stands for courage, the white stands for goodness, and the blue stands for justice.*)

4. Tell students to be ready to explain the main idea Aileen Fisher is suggesting in "Our Flag."

During Reading

1. This is a good poem for the students to practice for a performance at a Flag Day or Memorial Day celebration. In preparation, read the poem to the class, using voice inflection to emphasize the pride and emotion the author intends.

2. Allow the students to read the poem chorally with you several times, until you feel fluency has been reached.

3. Then have the group read the poem on their own, without your assistance. Encourage memorization, if possible. Add props and/or costumes for the performance if available.

After Reading

For discussion, ask the following question: "What is the main idea the author is suggesting?" (*Our flag is a symbol of freedom, and means even more as time goes by.*) Discuss recent events that make this true.

Reading Support

Highlight the words in the poem that contain the long *i* sound. Categorize and discuss the three spelling patterns that this sound represents (*-igh, -y, -i*). Break the class into three groups. In a specified amount of time, have each group list more words of their spelling pattern. (Students may use books or dictionary for help if time permits.) The group with the most correct responses wins!

Our Flag

Aileen Fisher

How bright our flag

against the <u>sky</u>

atop its flagpole

straight and _____.

How bright the red, the white, the <u>blue</u>,

with what they stand for

shining _____,

More meaningful

as years go <u>by</u> . . .

how bright, how bright,

the flag we _____.

Our Flag

Directions: Draw and color an illustration of the American flag as Aileen Fisher describes it. Label the following parts of the flag and tell for what they stand: the stars, the stripes, the red, the white, and the blue.

Skyscrapers
Rachel Field

Do skyscrapers ever grow tired

    Of holding themselves up high?

Do they ever shiver on frosty nights

    With their tops against the sky?

Do they feel lonely sometimes,

    Because they have grown so tall?

Do they ever wish they could lay right down

    And never get up at all?

"Skyscrapers," copyright 1924 by Yale University Press, from TAXIS AND TOADSTOOLS by Rachel Field. Used by permission of Random House Children's Books, a division of Random House, Inc.

Skyscrapers

Objectives

- Students will construct a drawing demonstrating understanding of descriptive details from the poem and other texts.

Materials

- a cloze copy of the poem (page 135)
- a highlighter and a pencil for each student
- several books from the library on skyscrapers
- chart paper or overhead

Before Reading

1. Discuss skyscrapers. For example, ask students the following: what are they, how are they built, where can they be found, some important ones the students know about.
2. Chart responses and save.
3. Ask if there are any specific skyscrapers they have seen or visited.
4. Collect several books from the library on skyscrapers. Assign one of these books to each of three or four small groups. Each group is given the task of finding more details on one of the above topics to add to the chart.
5. Students should be ready to answer the questions the author asks.

During Reading

1. Read the poem to the students twice, once as if they were statements, then a second time as questions.
2. Discuss the difference between the two readings. (*The students should notice that voice inflection changes when a question is being asked.*)
3. Divide the class into two groups. Have group one read line one, group two read line two, group one read line three, etc., until the entire poem is complete. Switch the starting group and read again.
4. Repeat as necessary.
5. End with a choral reading of the entire poem by the whole group.

After Reading

- Divide the group into pairs. In the groups, have them discuss how they would answer each of the author's questions. Discuss the conclusions they came to, and why they answered the way they did. What comparison is the author making? (*She is comparing skyscrapers to people who have feelings.*)
- Reread the poem again, this time substituting *tall people* for the word *skyscrapers* in the first line. Have the students discuss the questions the author asks again. Talk about the conclusions they came to. Under what conditions might each of the answers be "yes?"

Reading Support

Ask the students to highlight the following words in the poem: *tired, high, tops, tall, down, never.* Have them write an antonym above each of the highlighted words. Discuss and verify. Reread the poem substituting the antonyms. Does it make sense?

Skyscrapers
Rachel Field

Do skyscrapers ever grow tired

    Of holding themselves up <u>high</u>?

Do they ever shiver on frosty nights

    With their tops against the _____?

Do they feel lonely sometimes,

    Because they have grown so <u>tall</u>?

Do they ever wish they could lay right down

    And never get up at _____?

Skyscrapers

Directions: Draw a picture of yourself standing in the middle of New York or some other big city, surrounded by skyscrapers and other buildings. Use details from the poem and chart to help you. Write a caption to go with your picture and then explain how it feels to be there and why.

ART GALLERY

_____

(caption)

_____

_____

_____

_____

_____

_____

The Sun's Journey

Carolyn Sherwin Bailey

The sun is up so very long
Before a body's out,
He hurries through the dusk and dew
And garden paths about.

A little child may look at him
While lying still in bed,
And watch behind the window blind
His bobbing, yellow head.

From morn to noon and afternoon
He paces slowly round,
And warms the trees and all he sees,
And dries the dewy ground.

Sometimes he sits beside the door—
Sometimes upon the wall.
He stops and pats the tabby cats
And has a smile for all.

But when the day is near its end
And children nod and yawn,
With steps as far as giants' are
He strides across the lawn.

Beyond the fields he goes until,
Where meadows end you spy
A half his head and then instead
One winking, sleepy eye.

The Sun's Journey

Objectives

- Students will locate details describing "The Sun's Journey."
- Students will sequence these details in the correct order.

Materials

- a cloze copy of the poem (page 139)
- *The Sun is My Favorite Star* by Frank Asch (Harcourt, Inc., 2000), or another book containing information about the sun
- pencil and highlighter for each student
- overhead or board space

Before Reading

1. Ask students what they know about the sun. Where is it in the sky in the morning, at noon, and at night? In what other places can the sun be seen? Using the What I Know column of a Knowledge Chart (similar to the one below), log student responses.

The Sun

What I Know	What I Learned

2. Read *The Sun is My Favorite Star*, or another book about the sun, to the students.
3. Add information they learned in the What I Learned column.
4. Students are now ready to read "The Sun's Journey." They should be thinking about additional details they can add to the Knowledge Chart.

During Reading

1. Modeling good fluency, read the first line of the poem to your group. Have the students read the first line after you, echoing what you have read. Continue until the poem is complete.
2. Divide the class into six groups and assign each group a stanza of the poem. Have the groups practice reading their stanzas. Have group one present stanza one, while the rest of the class follows along. Continue with group two, etc., until all stanzas are presented.
3. Close with a group choral reading of the poem.

After Reading

- Highlight details that describe the sun. Are any of these already on the chart? What new ones can be added? Which details, in particular, pertain specifically to the journey the sun makes every day?
- Using student input, compose on separate sentence strips, details that describe the sun's daily journey. On each strip, include one fact about the sun and where it is located at specific times during the day: early morning, late morning, at noon, later in the afternoon, and at night, for example. Discuss its cyclical nature. (The sun travels in the same path day after day.) Scramble the sentence strips. Then with student help, rearrange them in sequential order. Add signal words where appropriate: *first, next, then, last,* etc., for example.

Reading Support

Break the class into small groups. Have each group generate rhyming words from one of the word families in the poem. Check and transfer to word cards; use for playing word games such as Concentration and Go Fish.

The Sun's Journey
Carolyn Sherwin Bailey

The sun is up so very long

Before a body's <u>out</u>,

He hurries through the dusk and dew

And garden paths _____.

A little child may look at him

While lying still in <u>bed</u>,

And watch behind the window blind

His bobbing, yellow _____.

From morn to noon and afternoon

He paces slowly <u>round</u>,

And warms the trees and all he sees,

And dries the dewy _____.

Sometimes he sits beside the door—

Sometimes upon the <u>wall</u>.

He stops and pats the tabby cats

And has a smile for _____.

But when the day is near its end

And children nod and <u>yawn</u>,

With steps as far as giants' are

He strides across the _____.

Beyond the fields he goes until,

Where meadows end you <u>spy</u>

A half his head and then instead

One winking, sleepy _____.

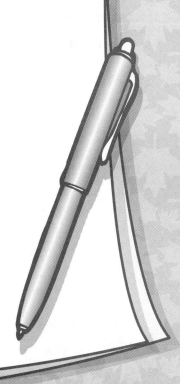

The Sun's Journey

Directions: Go back and read "The Sun's Journey" again. Which stanza is your favorite? Illustrate it below. Include as many details as you can from the stanza you chose in your picture. Then write a few sentences to explain what your illustration is about.

Poetry Projects

Junk Poetry

Here is a great way for students to get to know one another while engaging in a cooperative learning activity. First, group the students in groups of four or five. Have them contribute one or two small items and place them in the center of the table. Arrange these into a pleasing display. On 3" x 5" (8 cm x 13 cm) index cards or pieces of paper, have the students list one word per card that describes their grouping. Next, choose some word cards and arrange them to make a group poem. Extra words can be added, if desired. Students can share their poems with one another by moving from table to table as a group or have one student from each group share with the class about its poem.

Partner Poetry

Divide your class into teams of two. Partner one writes five or six questions that begin with the word "Why." At the same time, on a separate piece of paper, the second partner writes five or six answers beginning with "Because" without knowing what are the five or six questions. Then, the partners get together and re-write their questions and answers to form a partner poem. Some of the poems will turn out really silly, while others make quite a bit of sense! For extra fun, let the partners illustrate their partner poems.

Why does the ball roll? Because it is happy.

Why does the sun shine? Because it wears a coat.

Why did she call on you? Because he got a new goat.

Why can the elephant sing? Because it wears suspenders.

Why do mice eat cheese? Because it won't turn blue!

Poem Re-Writes

Write the first two lines of a poem. Have students brainstorm a list of words that rhyme with the last words in the lines. Then have them write one or two new lines to go with the first two.

On the first day of Christmas

My true love gave to me

A crumpet and a steaming pot of tea.

Poetry Projects

Magazine Poems

Instead of having your students make up their poems by writing with a pencil, provide magazines and let the class find their words by looking through the magazine pages. Have them cut and paste the words together to form their poems. Display the poems in the hallway or on a bulletin board.

Alphabetical Couplets

Combine two types of poetry to create a truly unique poem. Choose any two consecutive letters of the alphabet, for example O and P. The first line of the poem must begin with O. The second line must begin with P and end with a rhyme for the last word in the first line. Look at the example below.

> O is for orange, round and rough.
>
> P is for potato, fried and tough.

As a variation, the teacher assigns two letters to each pair. Then one partner writes the first line while the other partner writes the second line. Have students share their poems aloud.

As a challenge, ask students to write couplets relating to a similar topic for the whole alphabet. Pair letters together beginning with A and B, then C and D, etc. Be sure to choose broad topics such as animals, holidays, or sports to tie all of the couplets together.

Grab Bag Poems

Place one small item in a lunch sack. Prepare one for each student and fill with items such as cooking utensils (spatula, wood spoon, measuring cups, etc.); cleaning items (sponge, empty spray bottle, bar of soap, etc.); personal hygiene items (toothbrush, comb, washcloth, etc.); small toys (marbles, cars, rubber ball, etc.). Let each child choose a sack. He or she must write a poem about the object in the bag. (*Note:* It might be helpful to have children list two or three words that rhyme with their object before they begin to write. Grab bags may contain pictures rather than actual objects.)

Cause/Effect Poetry

Conduct an initial lesson in the concept of cause and effect. For example, a poem about a snowman with the sun shining would say that soon, due to the "cause" (the sun), the "effect" will be a melted snowman. Have your students write poetry that includes the cause and effect of an event as part of the poem.

Credits and Sources

Aldis, Dorothy. "Hiding," "No One Heard Him Call," and "The Sad Shoes." *All Together*. G.P. Putnam's Sons, 1928. Used by permission of G.P. Putnam's Sons, a division of Penguin Young Readers Group, A Member of Penguin Group (USA) Inc., 345 Hudson St., New York, NY 10014. All rights reserved.

Asquith, Herbert. "The Hairy Dog." *Pillicock Hill*. MacMillan, 1926.

Bailey, Carolyn Sherwin. "Toys," "The Sun's Journey," "The Naughty Boy," "Mother's Little Girl," and "The Good Night Sheep." *Stories and Rhymes for a Child*. Milton Bradley Co., 1909.

Dennis, Eleanor. "I Dreamed I Was a Snowman" and "March Wind." *Poetry Place Anthology*. Edgell Communications Inc., 1983. Reprinted by permission of Scholastic, Inc.

Evans, Helen Kitchell. "Little Joey." *Poetry Place Anthology*. Edgell Communications Inc., 1983. Reprinted by permission of Scholastic, Inc.

Field, Rachel. "I'd Like to Be A Lighthouse." *Taxis and Toadstools*. Doubleday, a Division of Random House, Inc, 1926. "Skyscrapers." *Taxis and Toadstools*. Yale University Press, 1924. Used by permission of Random House Children's Books, a division of Random House.

Fisher, Aileen. "As Soon as It's Fall," *Cricket in a Thicket*. Thomas Y Crowell, 1969. "Bluebird." *In the Woods, In the Meadow, In the Sky*. Thomas Y Crowell, 1967. "Our Flag." *Skip Around the Year*. Thomas Y Crowell, 1967. Used by permission of Marian Reiner for the Boulder Public Library Foundation.

Follen, Eliza Lee. "Do You Guess It Is I?" and "The Moon." *Poems by Mrs. Follen*. W. Crosby & Co., 1839.

Fyleman, Rose. "The Balloon Man" and "Very Lovely." *Fairies and Chimneys*. Doubleday, Doran & Co., 1920.

Credits and Sources

Gouled, Vivian. "Reading Books" and "With a Friend." *Poetry Place Anthology.* Edgell Communications Inc., 1983. Reprinted by permission of Scholastic, Inc.

Greenaway, Kate. "On the Bridge." *Marigold Garden.* Frederick Warne & Co. Ltd., 1885.

Hanna, Barbara. "Grandma's Cookie Jar." *Poetry Place Anthology.* Edgell Communications Inc., 1983. Reprinted by permission of Scholastic, Inc.

Lawrence, Helen Crooker. "Baby Sister." *Poetry Place Anthology.* Edgell Communications Inc., 1983. Reprinted by permission of Scholastic, Inc.

Lindsay, Vachel. "Little Turtle." *Collected Poems.* MacMillan, 1913.

Parker, Marion. "The Lost Balloon." *Poetry Place Anthology.* Edgell Communications Inc., 1983. Reprinted by permission of Scholastic, Inc.

Roberts, Elizabeth Madox. "Woodpecker." *Under the Tree.* B.W. Huebsch, Inc., 1922.

Sherman, Frank Dempster. "The Snow-Bird" and "A Real Santa Claus." *Little-Folk Lyrics.* Houghton Mifflin, 1897.

Stevenson, Robert Louis. "A Good Play" and "The Swing." *A Child's Garden of Verses and Underwoods.* Current Literature Publishing Co., 1910.